T0065761

NEW COVENANT LIBERTY FOR THE GENTILE BELIEVER

KENNETH BINKLEY, ThD

WESTBOW
PRESS®
A DIVISION OF THOMAS NELSON
& ZONDERVAN

This book is a work of non-fiction. Unless otherwise noted, the author and the publisher make no explicit guarantees as to the accuracy of the information contained in this book and in some cases, names of people and places have been altered to protect their privacy.

WestBow Press books may be ordered through booksellers or by contacting:

WestBow Press
A Division of Thomas Nelson & Zondervan
1663 Liberty Drive
Bloomington, IN 47403
www.westbowpress.com
844-714-3454

Because of the dynamic nature of the Internet, any web addresses or links contained in this book may have changed since publication and may no longer be valid. The views expressed in this work are solely those of the author and do not necessarily reflect the views of the publisher, and the publisher hereby disclaims any responsibility for them.

Any people depicted in stock imagery provided by Getty Images are models, and such images are being used for illustrative purposes only.
Certain stock imagery © Getty Images.

Unless otherwise noted, scripture taken from the New King James Version®. Copyright © 1982 by Thomas Nelson. Used by permission. All rights reserved.

Scripture marked (KJV) taken from the King James Version of the Bible.

Scripture quotations marked (ESV) are from The ESV® Bible (The Holy Bible, English Standard Version®), copyright © 2001 by Crossway, a publishing ministry of Good News Publishers. Used by permission. All rights reserved.

ISBN: 978-1-6642-7758-8 (sc)
ISBN: 978-1-6642-7760-1 (hc)
ISBN: 978-1-6642-7759-5 (e)

Library of Congress Control Number: 2022916723

Print information available on the last page.

WestBow Press rev. date: 10/21/2022

CONTENTS

ACKNOWLEDGMENTS

My appreciation is first and foremost to our loving Father who created us and sustains us all, then to all who have been faithful in ministering the Word of God, without apology. Such have been my teachers and counselors; from elementary Bible schoolteachers to devout and righteous ministers, the grace of God has reached even me. May Father honor, empower, and graciously reward them.

INTRODUCTION

For many Christians who glaze across the sacred scriptures, context and comprehension may evade them through unfamiliar ancient customs, contrasting covenants, and supposed contradictions; the covenant narrative has become distorted in modern Christianity, as its relevance is often misunderstood or ignored. Many in Christianity were taught about a loving Savior in Yeshua Hamashiach (Jesus Christ), His sacrifice, and yet we scarcely comprehend the plan and purpose of the Father, who ordered our redemption through various covenants to secure our redemption. Yehovah (God) predestined a plan, a purchase, and a purpose for us that we might be reconciled to Him (2 Cor. 5:19). He did not go about it without significant effort while concealing His salvation plan's mysteries through indirect series of events; we extract the truth and process of His intentions across the millennia, via biblical ancestors, obscure prophets, and hidden messages. This book is intended to provide a clear perspective for the bereft Gentile Christian and Messianic Hebrew who may be struggling with Mosaic Law dependencies, time periods, New versus Old Covenants, and their application as juxtaposed with the Good News, the liberty contained within the Gospel of Yeshua Hamashiach.

Denominationalism has clouded the Gospel with dubious theology, resigned to ear tickling, token phrases, and diluted Bible teaching to placate the hearer and keep church attendance up. Progressive heresies have infiltrated many religious organizations, having little to no regard for Yeshua Hamashiach (Jesus Christ) truth or His sacrifice through which He manifests His righteousness in us. Contrarily, some promote a return to contradictory aspects of the Law of Moses (a portion of Yehovah's instructions, teaching, or Torah), to assume control and profit with the perception of authority, while others support unitarianism, sin tolerance, sexual perversions, Satanism, abortion, and idolatry. Despite the mangling of the Gospel and the other obvious deceptions, there remains the truth of the Word of Yehovah and His provision for sanctification and holiness. In contrast, there is liberty derived through the Mosaic Covenant that is delivered through Yeshua Hamashiach's ministration of the New Covenant and the infilling of the Holy Spirit. All the righteous requirements of the Old Testament (OT) are contained in and satisfied within Yeshua's New Covenant. Unfortunately, many portions of Torah (instructions or teaching) are often conflated with the New Covenant and inferred as legally binding upon the Christian, and some are considered as no longer applicable; however, as we shall discover, many of the OT precepts (teachings) are already contained within the New Covenant, as embodied in Yeshua Hamashiach and Yehovah's preeminent instructions.

Navigating through the scriptures, we will reveal the plan of Yehovah's (God) salvation plan through its transition into the New Covenant, its power over sin, and rediscover a vitality for loving the Father. With the confusion surrounding multiple covenants and promises spanning six thousand years, how do we get there? This book provides a layman's pathway to understand those covenant hurdles, their progression from the Old Covenant (Mosaic) to the New Covenant, and addresses whether various tenets of the Mosaic Covenant remain incumbent on the New Covenant body.

This book does not reveal anything new that has not been written and read for multiple millennia. There are no grand revelations, dreams, or visions to excite the reader. There is, however, a captivating truth that will set many Christians free from denominational bondage critically selected from the Old Testament covenant. We will learn of Yehovah's intense desire to reconcile us, to bring us into His presence, to imbue us with a vibrant joy and thankful heart for His mercy and grace and of our liberation from misapplied and encumbering doctrines of men.

We will become acquainted with the Father in a more intimate fellowship, using His name, Yehovah, regularly to dispel the connotation of an unfeeling, distant, authoritarian ruler rather than the person who is the great I AM, your Redeemer, the one who formed you in your mother's womb (Ps. 139:13, Eccles. 11:5). Yehovah is our Father, our Abba, our heavenly, endearing Daddy. For some, these terms are too permissive, but how can it be that the God who died for you, knowing your sinful past, could possibly be repulsed by your affection? I encourage you to search out the scriptures and allow the Holy Spirit (Ruach Hakodesh) to guide your heart into the freedom that Yeshua Hamashiach (Jesus Christ) provides us.

> Be diligent to present yourself approved to God, a worker who does not need to be ashamed, rightly dividing the word of truth. (2 Tim. 2:15 NKJV)

My hope and prayer are that this book will supply a solid background of the dispensational, prophetic, and covenantal aspects of the Father's salvation plan as interwoven within His promises throughout the historical covenants that He made to ordinary men—men of faith, failure, hope, and all things still common to us today. We will confirm our Father's faithfulness to us, whose desire has always been to create a beautiful existence and to give life to His sons and daughters. We journey through scriptures to see how the Word of Yehovah (God) reveals His divine purpose through interstitial promises and revelations to set His children at liberty, to discover His unbounding affection toward us, and to enable us to reciprocate our love toward Him without restraint. This book will serve as a faith guide, grounded in Yehovah's Word; a Father's passport to our freedom from fear and bondage, granting us passage to His true Sabbath Day rest.

> What man is he that feareth the Lord? him shall he teach in the way that he shall choose. His soul shall dwell at ease; and his seed shall inherit the earth. The secret of the Lord is with them that fear him; and he will shew them his covenant. (Ps. 25:12–14 NKJV)

What an extraordinary and marvelous promise for us! For those who love Yehovah, He has promised to teach; their souls shall be at ease, their children shall inherit the earth, and His secret covenant He will show to them! We have a glorious promise here and a glorious responsibility to walk in the revelation of the covenant He is revealing in this book. Covenants were not just for history or just for Abraham and Moses; they were established with a purpose to reconcile mankind back to Yehovah (God). Covenants were established for you, your children, and for their seed. We must walk in and share the freedoms that are in Christ Jesus, our New Covenant High Priest.

CHAPTER 1

CHRISTIAN LIBERTY

The spiritual climate today is marked by mass media events, concerts, entertainment, and flashy preachers, resulting in foundationally weak and confused believers. This book is written for those who struggle in their Christian faith with the overtures and persuasions of some religious figures and denominations who employ a nuanced twisting of scriptures to control and manipulate the body of Jesus Christ (a.k.a. Yeshua Hamashiach). The Mosaic Covenant and its commands are brought into the light of grace to reveal their concealed intent. Some commandments, as we will discover, have been set aside (Heb. 10:9) from the believer, while others are pleasantly folded into the New Covenant of Yeshua Hamashiach. When Yehovah (God) established the Mosaic Covenant through Moses, the Gentile was not a recipient or attendant of that Law (a.k.a. the Torah, Pentateuch, or Mosaic Covenant). It was not given to the Gentile, and Yehovah did not address the Gentile to abide by its laws; it was by invitation only via an exodus. Otherwise, they would have become grafted into the Mosaic system and no longer been considered a Gentile.

Why, therefore, are selective Old Testament (OT) commandments routinely stressed upon by some as presumed New Testament (NT) legalisms, as incumbent upon the body of Yeshua Hamashiach (Jesus Christ) today, and whether they have they been incorporated into the New Covenant or not?

We first need to understand that the foundational principles for the Ten Commandments were in order long before the Mosaic Covenant was given. Heaven is ruled by the same God who gave instruction for conduct to Adam and his descendants and who gave Moses the Torah (instructions or law); all proceeded from the same throne. The descendants of Adam knew Yehovah's natural law and what Yehovah desired of them, even as Cain knew hatred and murder were against Yehovah's will, as does today's non-Christian; it is written in our conscience just as surely as is our desire to breathe. Those who followed Adam knew, even as we know today, what is morally right and what is wrong. So precisely what did the Mosaic Covenant introduce, and why did Yehovah wait 2,500 years after the creation of Adam to institute it? The Old Testament commandments, having not yet been given, could have no legal bearing on those persons who preexisted the Mosaic Law, nor did it bear upon the unbelieving Gentile. The righteous instructions were conveyed by Yehovah to Adam, whose children then conveyed God's righteous instructions, whatever their content, to his descendants up until Moses; it was not written in stone but on hearts, from generation to generation. They did not have the written Torah (meaning instructions) that we today refer to as the Old Testament. They kept the oral commandments that they passed from father to son over that span of 2,500 years, prior to the Mount Sinai covenant (Mosaic Covenant/OT). But again, the Mosaic Covenant would not have been in force, as Yehovah had not yet given it. Only later would Moses write the first five books of the Old Covenant, the Pentateuch.

Yeshua Hamashiach was crucified as the sacrificial Lamb of Yehovah 1,500 years after the writing of the Mosaic Covenant. How could the Levitical priest system as prescribed under that structure then continue? And if it did persist, how might it have changed?

> For the priesthood being changed, of necessity there is also
> a change of the law. (Heb. 7:12 NKJV)

We will investigate the clear distinctions provided in the pre-Law, the OT (Torah, Mosaic, or Aaronic Law), and New Covenant dispensations.

As we go through these promises and covenants, keep in mind that the Gentile did not have the fundamental, exhaustive religious teaching that the Hebrew children received. They wandered in darkness, just as many professed Christians and unbelievers do today. Nonetheless, the purpose of Yehovah has always been to redeem those of humanity who would be willing to accept His grace (Isa. 56:3–8), wrapped up in mystery, as a part of His plan of redemption. How our Father has chosen to bring about His plan of salvation is certainly beyond our comprehension. He had a purpose for us better than that of sons and daughters, as you will see.

The whole point of a New Covenant is to do something new. Many of us have heard the preacher proclaim that the Lord is doing a new thing today; well, that new thing is called the New Covenant. Unfortunately, some preachers do not stray far from their prescribed orthodoxy and do not get around to explaining specifically why we needed a New Covenant, what it released us from, its foundation within the Mosaic Law, or its preeminent predecessor. Yeshua adhered dutifully to the Mosaic Law during His earthly ministry. He taught and interacted with the people in strict compliance with all its requirements and prophecies, up to and through His crucifixion, which established the demarcation from the Old Covenant, an ordained time of reformation.

> And fleshly ordinances imposed until the time of reformation. (Heb. 9:10 NKJV)

Herein lies the culmination of the Old Covenant and the institution of the New Covenant; this is immensely significant and vital to our relationship with the Father and our understanding of that relationship.

Yehovah (God) has proclaimed that He is taking away the old so that He can bring in the new. Referencing Jesus in Hebrews 10:9 (NKJV), the scripture says,

> Then He said, "Behold, I have come to do Your will, O God." He takes away the first that He may establish the second.

What precisely was Yeshua (Jesus) talking about? It was not only the fact that He came to be the sacrificial Lamb of Yehovah but also that He came to fulfill the Mosaic Covenant and to set it aside (Heb. 7:18 ESV), or as referenced in the New King James Version, to annul it. There is much disagreement on whether the Mosaic Covenant was terminated or canceled, neither of which can be true, as Yeshua fulfilled it, and by so doing, He created one new man from the two disparate groups— Hebrew and Gentile—within Himself and abolished the enmity that had existed between them that was spurred on by the law of commandments contained in ordinances (Eph. 2:15–16). Thereafter, he annulled and/or set the Mosaic Covenant aside. There remained nothing in its content to be completed by Him except the eternal promises that God had made to the fathers (Luke 1:72) and to the captives (Rom. 11:28, Eph. 4:8, 1 Pet. 3:19) who previously lived under that covenant, as well as those who still choose to do so.

> For as many as have sinned without law will also perish without law, and as many as have sinned in the law will be judged by the law. (Rom. 2:12 NKJV)

Just as the pagan and Gentile will be judged in accordance with their natural moral compass, so will the Hebrew and Gentile who desire to justify themselves within the context of the Mosaic Covenant or Gentile/pagan persuasion. Similarly, those who accept Yeshua Hamashiach as their Messiah and His atoning sacrifice will be judged according to Yeshua's work on the cross via their imputed, indisputable righteous standing before God (2 Cor. 5:17, 21).

The whole point of the revelation of Yeshua Hamashiach as the Messiah was to reveal the God Man as the Savior who would fulfill those covenants to the Hebrew people as prophesied by Zacharias (Luke 1:72–75), who were enemies for the Gentiles' sake, and join them with the Gentile believers in Christ Jesus, thus creating one new man.

> Concerning the gospel, they are enemies for your sake, but concerning the election they are beloved for the sake of the fathers. For the gifts and the calling of God are irrevocable. For as you were once disobedient to God, yet have now obtained mercy through their disobedience, even so these also have now been disobedient, that through the mercy shown you they also may obtain mercy. For God has

committed them all to disobedience, that He might have
mercy on all. (Rom. 11:28–32 NKJV)

Even as old wineskins cannot contain new wine, of necessity, new
wineskins must be used, as the old wineskins (Mosaic Law), having become
hardened through the fermentation process, were incapable of expanding,
and the new wine fermentation would cause the old skins to burst. The
presence of the Holy Spirit (Ruach HaKodesh), the new wine, would disrupt
the theological bent of the Hebrew children, who were bound by the Old
Covenant, as the apostle Paul can attest, and who would temporarily become
enemies of the Gospel for our sake (Rom. 11:28). Howbeit, Yehovah, in His
riches of mercy, has also provided them with the same eternal forgiveness of
their sins as afforded the Gentile through the New Covenant.

Yeshua Hamashiach (Christ Jesus) died to set us free and to burst
old wineskins. The Old Covenant cords that bound the Jews by rituals—
commands of purification, service, and conduct—were needful for their
instruction and sanctification of the people until the Messiah could come,
a covenantal reformation (Heb. 9:10). Their blindness, however, prevented
them from recognizing Him, and they stumbled at His coming. Yeshua
became their stumbling stone, and they rejected the very Messiah they had
long been awaiting.

Some Christian teachers and denominations misappropriate various
tenets of the OT and Torah to compel compliance from believers. As we
examine these three dispensations, some of those misguided teachings will
be put to rest as their intent comes to light from what once were thought to
be disparate covenantal relationships, though now they can be understood
as being built one upon the other, that mercy might be shown to all (Rom.
11:32).

The New Covenant's consummation at the cross supplied our
deliverance from a works-oriented salvation based in the Mosaic Covenant.
It is vital that the believer in Christ Jesus understands that the Mosaic Law
was the foundation of the New Covenant's legal bearing, yet prior to both
was the promise that Yehovah made to Abram. Consequently, that which
was born upon the Mosaic Covenant required its subsequent setting aside
of that Law, that the Law of the Spirit of Life could manifest through the
New Covenant (Rom. 8:2).

For you have not come to the mountain that may be touched and that burned with fire, and to blackness and darkness and tempest, and the sound of a trumpet and the voice of words, so that those who heard it begged that the word should not be spoken to them anymore. (Heb. 12:18–19 NKJV)

And so terrifying was the sight that Moses said, "I am exceedingly afraid and trembling.") But you have come to Mount Zion and to the city of the living God, the heavenly Jerusalem, to an innumerable company of angels, to the general assembly and church of the firstborn who are registered in heaven, to God the Judge of all, to the spirits of just men made perfect, to Jesus the Mediator of the New Covenant, and to the blood of sprinkling that speaks better things than that of Abel. (Heb. 12:21–24 NKJV)

Beloved, we are the recipients of God's eternal mercies, His Holy Spirit who purifies our lives unto perfection, and given a new Mediator for our benefit apart from the Law of Moses and its terror.

CHAPTER 2

WHAT ABOUT THE LAW?

Moreover, the law entered that the offense might abound. But where sin abounded, grace abounded much more, so that as sin reigned in death, even so grace might reign through righteousness to eternal life through Jesus Christ our Lord.
—ROMANS 5:20 (NKJV)

The Law was given not to make us perfect but to illuminate our limitations and imperfections. What was Yehovah thinking? Didn't He already know what a mess we were? Of course, He did. The problem was, and still is, we do not recognize our own weaknesses and shortcomings; therefore, the Law's intent was to reveal and convince us of our depravity and woeful, desperate condition. The Law entered that the offense might abound!

This scripture rattled my religious understanding. I supposed that accepting Yeshua Hamashiach was sufficient, and in the simplest of terms, it is. However, the revelation of why Yehovah enacted the Mosaic Law with its intent to create greater offense, an acceleration of iniquity, was quite foreign and disturbing. Like most Christians, as a child, the acceptance of Yehovah's grace was elemental and beneficial enough for conscience's sake. It was a gospel with childhood Jesus stories for most of my upbringing, where the Hebraic roots of Christianity remained untaught and assumed peaceable as to their application. Still, those lingering questions remained; what about the Law of Moses? Was it now irrelevant? How and when did the Old Covenant terminate? What constituted the expiration, change, or transfer to the New Covenant? What are the benefits of the New Covenant? What was the benefit of knowing basic Old Testament (OT) covenants and their history? And how did we Gentiles come to receive Yeshua when so much of the Bible is directed specifically toward the Hebrew, or so we were taught?

Bypassing OT doctrine and functions of the priesthood were convenient for most Sunday school classes. As Christians, we simply did not bother with diving into the covenant details. For most of us, the whole Levitical sacrificial system is difficult to piece together, with its washings, blood offerings, incense offerings, grain offerings, holy days, and many other religious observances. All of them, however, were needful, authored, and sacred before Yehovah. We would do well to engage in their symbolic practices during the Hebrew holy days and feast days as a remembrance and to embrace an understanding of their significance as they continue to focus, even today, the light of redemption upon Yeshua Hamashiach.

Unfortunately, that inattentiveness of the Mosaic system and its covenantal precedence has led to some theological mangling of that covenant and has allowed legalism, either by hook or crook, into New Covenant theology, the very issue the apostle Paul was routinely persecuted for by the Pharisees and Sadducees and for which he labored against intensely. Moreover, without a rudimentary understanding as to why the Mosaic Law was provisioned by Yehovah, we cannot adequately understand the significant separation from the OT legal narrative and its form of transference from the temporary blood atonement ascribed under the Law to the eternal, most sacred and holiest blood atonement of the Son of Yehovah. These two covenants are foundational to the transference of Yehovah's redemptive work from a legal works-based salvation to the message of the Gospel of grace through Yeshua Hamashiach. Without a clear understanding of the parameters of each covenant, the Christian mindset could easily be misled back into several forms of legalistic bondage (e.g., circumcision, tithes, and holy days). Unfortunately, this has been the case with several New Testament freedoms. So who needed to know about this concept of "that the offense might abound"? The answer is clear; we all do.

Seldom, if ever, is the Mosaic Covenant referred to in Christian circles as a ministry of death. If it had, I suppose there would be far fewer folks returning to the meeting house the following week. However, the apostle Paul poignantly describes it that way:

> But if the ministry of death, written and engraved on stones, was glorious, so that the children of Israel could not look steadily at the face of Moses because of the glory of his countenance, which glory was passing away. (2 Cor. 3:7 NKJV)

Here, we see that Paul confirms that the Law of Moses began passing away as soon as Moses had received it. Then in 2 Corinthians 3:9 (NKJV), Paul calls it "the ministry of condemnation." Well, if that does not get you all fired up to go to church, I do not know what else would. Our Christian construct of the Old Covenant has been glazed over and misrepresented; I suppose because someone felt Yehovah needed a little help in the public relations department. But here it is, sin was to abound via the ministries of death and condemnation, and now modern-day Christians want to go back to the Law? (Sarcasm mine.) Moving a little farther down the chapter, 2 Corinthians 3:11 (NKJV) further defines the passing of the Mosaic Law:

> For if what is passing away was glorious, what remains is much more glorious. (2 Cor. 3:11 NKJV)

And once again, in case you missed it:

> Unlike Moses, who put a veil over his face so that the children of Israel could not look steadily at the end of what was passing away. (2 Cor. 3:13 NKJV)

Apparently, they could already see the beginning of it passing away; the glory of the Law of Moses was already fading. Now, having just received the Law, they are looking for its passing, as its glory was to be eclipsed by that of the New Covenant. Believe it or not, some folks continue to deny the authority of the Word of Yehovah in this transition, and that to their own loss.

Galatians 3:19 provides us the purpose of the Law:

> What purpose then does the law serve? It was added
> because of transgressions, till the Seed should come to
> whom the promise was made. (Gal. 3:19 NKJV)

The Law was not Yehovah's initial design; though He knew beforehand of its necessity, it was added to His plan. Why was it added? Because sin had become so rampant that prohibitions were required as a deterrent to lawlessness. They lived without Torah, without instruction. Have you ever had children for a day and not given them rules and guidelines? It's a guaranteed disaster. Yehovah did not add the Law as punishment to beat us into obedience; He added it to persuade good behavior and to dissuade us from corruption and eternal loss. Jump to Galatians 3:23, 25, and the Law was our schoolmaster, our tutor. Our failure to keep it was intentional, designed to bring us to a point of desperation in the acknowledgment of our sin and to recognize our need for a Savior—to bring us to Yeshua Hamashiach! The Law was not introduced to finally declare that murder, lying, stealing, and fornication were wrong; they had always been sinful. The Law's purpose was to provide the groundwork for a legal and just reclamation of the fallen seed of Adam through the promised Messiah, the Son of God. His presentation mandated a holy covenant by which He could come into the world.

Yehovah's providential plan did not begin with the book of Matthew; there were about four thousand years of history before Yeshua Hamashiach came to earth as the Lamb of Yehovah, which provides the backdrop for the Father's plan of redemption to unfold. From the time of Adam to Abraham were 2,070 years, and then another 430 years before Moses led the children of Israel out of Egypt, which brings us to about 2,500 years since Adam's creation. Then, there is about 1,500-year span from the giving of the Law of Moses to the coming of the Messiah. To understand some basic chronology of events, we need to understand that there was no Mosaic Law for the first 2,500 years or so. Their guidance and instruction were given by Yehovah Yehovah to faithful men of the line of Seth, passed on orally, pre-literacy, through his descendants to the time of Noah, then Shem, and so on until we eventually get to the days of Abraham, some 2,070 years removed from the creation of Adam.

A rough chronology would be as follows:

+ Creation of Adam—zero years, 4000 BC/BCE (Before Common Era)
+ Adam to Abraham—2,070 years, approximately 1930 BC/BCE
+ Abraham to Moses—430 years, approximately 1500 BC/BCE
+ Moses to Christ Jesus—1,500 years, approximately 0 BC/BCE
+ Messiah Yeshua Hamashiach to present day—2,022 years / 2022 BC/BCE

Whenever Yehovah says anything, it is an absolute promise and truth.

> "So shall My word be that goes forth from My mouth; It shall not return to Me void, but it shall accomplish what I please, and it shall prosper in the thing for which I sent it." (Isa. 55:11 NKJV)

There were several promises and covenants before the Abrahamic covenant, such as the Adamic, Noahic, and a few after Abraham's; Mosaic, Davidic, Solomon, and, of course, the New or Messianic covenant, which entails them all. Nonetheless, we will focus primarily on the Mosaic and New Covenant, as they both have their anchor in the promises that Yehovah made to Abram. Abraham, as he is later called by Yehovah after the sign of circumcision is pronounced, is the father of both the Gentile promise and the Hebrew promise.

> Now the Lord had said to Abram: "Get out of your country, From your family And from your father's house, To a land that I will show you. I will make you a great nation; I will bless you And make your name great; And you shall be a blessing. I will bless those who bless you, And I will curse him who curses you; And in you all the families of the earth shall be blessed." (Gen. 12:1–3 NKJV)

God's promise was to all the families of the earth. Israel did not yet exist. Abram was a wandering, faithful Gentile and not an Israelite.

Yehovah made a promise to Abraham long before the Law of Moses was written. Another 430 years passed before the Law was given to Moses on Mt. Sinai and the children of Israel were constrained thereby. The Gentile peoples were generally despised by the Hebrew nation and ignored during the Mosaic Laws tenure, though Yehovah did promise Abram to bless all families through him (Gen. 12:3). Howbeit, Gentiles were invited to keep the Laws of Yehovah at any time and be grafted into the faith through obedience, and Yehovah would bless them eternally for their devotion (Isa. 56:3+). Comparatively, this puts us in mind of Cornelius, a Gentile centurion at Caesarea, whom Peter visited and witnessed to. Peter received directions in a vision of Yehovah's acceptance of things previously considered as unclean to eat, and of peoples previously considered unclean and uncircumcised. Through Peter's vision, Yehovah spoke clearly of His acceptance of Christ Jesus's fulfillment of the Mosaic Law and the initiation of the New Covenant when He poured out the Holy Spirit on all the Gentiles in Cornelius's house. Gentiles receiving the Holy Spirit was an extreme faith-challenging event that the Hebrew people would have to either accept or reject, as only Israelites had received the Holy Spirit on the Day of Pentecost; they assumed it a strictly Hebrew anointing. This outpouring became the hallmark of heightened debate and discontent among many Hebrews, especially the religious attendees of the temple in Jerusalem, whose holy of holies had recently been rendered useless by Yehovah himself. Certainly, a quandary had arisen in the Hebrew faith!

The Mosaic Law gave specific instruction for the nation of Israel to keep, that the blessings of Yehovah would continue to rest upon them. The Mosaic Covenant provided promises of blessings and curses in Leviticus chapter 26. When they rebelled and did not keep the Mosaic Covenant, Yehovah would lift His hand from them and allow their enemies to punish them. Likewise, when they repented and kept His Law, they would be restored, prosper, and excel against their enemies. We will come back to review some aspects of the Mosaic Covenant, the tutor and schoolmaster, but for now we need to understand that the Mosaic Law was an intermediary covenant until a more perfect New Covenant could be instated.

As Gentiles were not a large focus of the Mosaic Covenant, their inclusion into the plan of redemption does not occur significantly until after the crucifixion of Yeshua Hamashiach, the Lamb of Yehovah who takes away the sin of the world. As New Testament Christians, our primary focus tends to focus on that four-thousand-year mark after the creation of Adam, at Christ Jesus's birth; hence why so many Christians have little knowledge of Old Testament theology. Despite our limited knowledge, we began our faith journey much like Abraham did back in Genesis 12. We believe in the promise that Yehovah has made, the same way Abraham believed in the promise of Yehovah that all nations of the earth would be blessed in him. We, like Abraham, can choose to believe the Father's promises of His Messiah, the Seed, as our Redeemer, just as many of the Hebrew children believed in Him. The Jewish peoples looked forward to their promised Messiah's coming, while we Gentiles look back at the Messiah's life, death, and resurrection as fulfillment of Old Testament prophecies. Both classes of people require faith in a mysterious and fascinating plan of redemption!

So, we begin today, some 6022 +/- years removed from the time of the creation of Adam, with a similar faith much like Abraham's. We believe Yehovah!

CHAPTER 3

TWO COVENANTS, ONE BODY

Ephesians 2:15 (NKJV) states, "Having abolished in His flesh the enmity, that is, the law of commandments contained in ordinances, so as to create in Himself one new man from the two, thus making peace." There can be no doubt that the Law of commandments, the teachings of the prophets, were holy and pure; however, man was not, as he could not be, and was without hope due to man's propensity for sin and waywardness. What was this desire to sin that Adam succumbed to, that Lucifer succumbed to? Whatever its premise, Father devised a fail-proof plan of redemption to secure us in His own person. Thus, Christ Jesus came to fulfill the Law, to satisfy its demand of perfection and justice. The Law was the source that created offense between the Father's holiness and us. Christ Jesus, as the new High Priest, instituted a New Covenant through His own blood, bringing forth a new law through grace, the Law of the Spirit of Life (Rom. 8:2), the fulfillment of God's promise to Abram that would forever redeem and protect us.

The Father needed a plan to address the following needs:

+ How to obtain a redemption of humanity while also paying the penalty for their sin? However, since there was no righteous person left on the earth after the sin of Adam, "Who could He send to atone for their transgression and suffer the penalty of death?"
+ How could He insert a perfect sacrifice into the lineage of humanity without that righteous one's holiness being diminished by the

ravages of sin yet uphold the stringent commandments required to obtain redemption of man?

+ How could Yehovah qualify humanity in the simplest of transactions that anyone who believed in His plan could be saved, and how to safeguard them from falling away again?

+ What was this promise that Yehovah made, to make in Himself those who were under the Law and the Gentiles into one new man?

First, we have the promise from Yehovah in Genesis 3:15 of the promised Seed of the woman who would bruise the head of the serpent. And later in Genesis 12:3, when Yehovah made a promise to Abraham that he would be a blessing to all nations in Genesis 17:4 and,

> That the blessing of Abraham might come on the Gentiles through Jesus Christ, that we might receive the promise of the Spirit through faith. (Gal. 3:14 NKJV)

Secondly, we have inserted into the timeline of redemption, 2,500 years after the Fall of Adam, the giving of the Mosaic Law at Mount Sinai, Exodus chapters 20–24, often referred to as the First Covenant, as the foundation from which a greater covenant could be established. (See Heb. 7:12)

> But now He has obtained a more excellent ministry, inasmuch as He is also Mediator of a better covenant, which was established on better promises. (Heb. 8:6 NKJV)

A covenant that provided the means necessary to interject the Lamb of Yehovah into the lineage of humanity, with one who could overcome all temptation.

Thirdly, there is the consummation of the New Covenant through the blood sacrifice of Yeshua Hamashiach, that by faith in His name and atoning sacrifice would provide the necessary requirement for salvation to all who would believe in Him and through whom the gift of the Holy Spirit could be poured out to keep them from transgression and provide unrestrained access and communion with the Father.

Yehovah's promise was much more than a gesture of friendship but of an incredibly special gift of being one with Him, to always dwell in His presence by being one with Messiah and fellowship through the Holy Spirit. It was a promise of restoration of the Father's original desire to fellowship with us, His children. O how He has longed for His wayward people! We have neglected the truth of His passion toward us, as stated in the all too familiar verse:

> For God so loved the world that He gave His only begotten
> Son, that whoever believes in Him should not perish but
> have everlasting life. (John 3:16 NKJV)

Father has made a way for all to come to Him, sins atoned for, past forgotten, promises of life eternal, if only we would humble ourselves and come to Him.

> Now to Abraham and his Seed were the promises made.
> He does not say, "And to seeds," as of many, but as of one,
> "And to your Seed," who is Christ. (Gal. 3:16 NKJV)

We see that Jesus Christ is the Seed to whom the promise was made; a promise to Abram that was initially promised in the garden before the serpent, the woman, and her Seed, to be reaffirmed to Abram 2070 +/- years later, 430 years prior to the law being given to Moses. There was a long span of time from the garden event until Yehovah made a successive promise to Abram. The Law also did not annul the previous promise Yehovah made to Abraham.

> For if the inheritance is of the law, it is no longer of promise;
> but God gave it to Abraham by promise. (Gal. 3:17 NKJV)

The promise was not based on the law! Why? Yehovah's promise was based on Yehovah's desire to redeem mankind through the Seed; that is Yeshua Hamashiach. So, we see that apart from the promise, there was added the Mosaic Law to accommodate the Messiah's appointment and purpose toward salvation. Long before the Law was given, Yehovah had a plan to redeem man from his fallen state, apart from the dictums of the Mosaic Law, yet founded on its demand for sanctification, justice, and holiness; a wondrous reconciliation of both Jew and Gentile into one body of Christ through grace.

> But after faith has come, we are no longer under a tutor. (Gal. 3:25 NKJV)

The Law was the schoolmaster, the teacher, and our liberation is from the tenets of the Law, not just the Decalogue or the Ten Commandments but the whole embodiment of the Book of the Law, which was laid beside the ark of the covenant, wherein lay all the instructions to the priesthood and instructions for the nation.

> Take this Book of the Law and put it beside the ark of the covenant of the Lord your God, that it may be there as a witness against you; for I know your rebellion and your stiff neck. (Deut. 31:26 NKJV)

Again, the Book of the Law was a witness against them, a ministry of death, not for them, because He foreknew they would rebel and not keep it. It does not appear that Yehovah had much confidence in mortal man, only that He knew that mankind would sin perpetually without a righteous intervention.

If we judge ourselves honestly, we know our present-day obedience to the commandments of God are at times a struggle and that if required to meet compliance with the Law of Moses and the Book of the Law, we may well have little idea where to start, much less be any more successful than the Hebrew children. Thankfully, Yehovah did not leave us in our destitute condition. He provided us a way of escape.

> For Christ is the end of the law for righteousness to everyone who believes. (Rom. 10:4 NKJV)

If we believe in Yeshua Hamashiach, the Law has been ended for us. It remains therefore that there is nothing else that we are to do, or to work, to acquire that righteousness. He has already done all that can be done. The question before us today is the same as was before the Hebrews of Yeshua's day, "Do we believe in His atonement for our sins or not?"

> For you are all sons of God through faith in Christ Jesus. (Gal. 3:26 NKJV)

Jesus asked the Father for this very union:

> "That they all may be one, as You, Father, are in Me, and I in You; that they also may be one in Us, that the world may believe that You sent Me." (John 17:21 NKJV)

It was abundantly clear that the way to righteousness was not going to be accomplished by man's adherence to the Old Covenant; therefore, Yehovah made a way toward righteousness through Messiah for us, if we would only seek Him (Matt. 6:33).

> Who also made us sufficient as ministers of the New Covenant, not of the letter but of the Spirit; for the letter kills, but the Spirit gives life. But if the ministry of death, written and engraved on stones, was glorious, so that the children of Israel could not look steadily at the face of Moses because of the glory of his countenance, which glory was passing away, how will the ministry of the Spirit not be more glorious? (2 Cor. 3:6–8 NKJV)

Remember that sin was to increase under the Law, which included the Decalogue, or Ten Commandments; however, the Spirit of Life does not exempt us from righteous living or give us license to sin wantonly, as it dishonors the Father and will continue to bring His correction, or His wrath if we are recalcitrant. The Spirit of Life, the Holy Spirit of Yehovah, empowers us to keep what I refer to as the preeminent Law (Matt. 22:37–40) to honor Yehovah in all things by seeking, learning, and keeping our love fixed on Him, thereby keeping all that the Law and prophets were trying to teach us. We will touch more on this subject later.

So how was the ministration of the Spirit in the New Covenant to be more glorious than that of the glory at Mt. Sinai? The glory of Mt. Sinai was in physical display awe and terror, but it brought forth the redemptive Passover's consummation, which atoned for the sins of the believer, and it brought forth the promise of the Holy Spirit (Mark 1:8) to assist in the sanctification process of the believer (1 Pet. 1:22, Rom. 12:1+), who imbues us with power over sin and all the power of the enemy (Luke 10:19) and who leads us into truth (John 16:13). The same power that resurrected Yeshua Hamashiach from the dead (Rom. 8:10–11) now lives within the believer to direct and recreate us in His likeness. This is true liberty!

Yeshua Hamashiach satisfied the requirements of the Old Covenant (Mt. Sinai) and opened the door for the New Covenant by being birthed through the Mosaic Law; He consummated the New Covenant by the shedding of His blood, satiating the righteous wrath of Yehovah and baptizing his Hebrew and Gentile followers with His life-giving Holy Spirit (Mark 1:8, John 1:33).

CHAPTER 4

GENTILE BELIEVERS

We begin with the apostle Paul's letter to the Galatians, where some Messianic Hebrews had relocated during the dispersion from persecution (2 Pet. 1:1), and the larger Greek-speaking Gentile group that lived there who were unfamiliar with much of the teaching of the Torah, the first five books of the Old Testament written by Moses. The Galatians had much to learn, and Paul had instructed them on prior missionary trips of the salvation for all men through Yeshua Hamashiach's redemptive work on the cross. Their comprehension was akin to the modern-day Christian who also knows little of ancient Hebrew customs, their patriarchal system, the Torah's legal structure, dietary laws, and cleanliness doctrine. Many of the Galatians were converted pagans and sinners who had limited or no knowledge of the Mosaic Covenant or their Hebrew Messiah, but what they did know was their awareness of human imperfection, deities and idolatry, a desperate acknowledgment of sin and their need for holiness. They had been drawn in by Yehovah, recognizing their own incapacity of achieving sanctification by human merit and idolatrous worship; something was missing. Pagan worship was widespread and provided a sensual, worldly, and culturally acceptable alternative to squelch one's conscience for a time; they had been blind, hungry, and naked, but now they had received the Gospel of Yeshua, a hope for righteousness and eternal life. Today, many Christians struggle spiritually, performing religious rigor and duty to impress men, equally blind and destitute from religious dogma and false doctrine, thirsting, dying at the well of Yehovah. Partial knowledge of the holy scriptures produces partial truth and misunderstanding, diminishing the work that Christ Jesus completed for us by His work on the cross.

> O foolish Galatians! Who has bewitched you that you should not obey the truth before whose eyes Jesus Christ was clearly portrayed among you as crucified? This only I want to learn from you: Did you receive the Spirit by the works of the law, or by the hearing of faith? (Gal. 3:1–2 NKJV)

As previously stated, the Galatians knew little regarding the Mosaic Law; they consisted of a mix of Gentile Greeks, pagans, and deists, as was common through all the Gentile cities, along with Messianic Hebrews. Now, after receiving the Gospel of Yeshua Hamashiach and the baptism of the Holy Spirit, they were being misled by some Hebrew teachers who were instructing them to obey requirements of the Mosaic Law, in this case, specifically that all males should be circumcised. Doing so would relegate the newborn believers into obeying all the Mosaic Law, as it is a works-based covenant.

> But that no one is justified by the law in the sight of God is evident, for "the just shall live by faith." Yet the law is not of faith, but "the man who does them shall live by them. (Gal. 3:11–12 NKJV)

Regarding the Law, Yehovah promised to bless them only if they kept all His commands. Conversely, He also promised to punish them if they did not. Paul reminds them of this:

> Cursed is everyone who does not continue in all things which are written in the book of the law, to do them. (Gal. 3:10 NKJV)

Paul's admonishment was to keep them from circumventing the work that Yeshua Hamashiach's blood atonement purchased for them through the New Covenant. Any Mosaic Law observed as compliance to the Mosaic

Covenant—animal sacrifice, observance of holy days, tithes, feast days, and so on—would cancel out any faith they may have had in the atoning blood of the Lord Jesus. Though many of those observances can still be observed today, a Passover (Seder) dinner in honor of the cultural significance and historical value, a freewill tithe, honoring the Sabbath, or even observing the rites of the Temple ceremony for educational purposes are wonderful reminders and of significant benefit to understand their prophetic influence or how the covenants transitioned; however, they should cease being observed as a component in trying to be justified by keeping the Mosaic Law. Yeshua's New Covenant provides us salvation by faith through Yehovah's grace (Eph. 2:8), though it, too, is contingent on our faith to believe it. That faith will be demonstrated by our love and thanksgiving for His mercy, resulting in our obedience and faithfulness to His will.

> For by one offering He has perfected forever those who are being sanctified. (Heb. 10:14 NKJV)

There is a subsequent working out of our faith (Phil. 2:12) that is not sedentary but a continuous service in seeking the Father's will, a process of sanctification, a renewal of the mind and soul (1 Pet. 1:15–16, Matt. 6:33). Just as Jesus's admonition to Peter, "You follow me" (John 21:22 NKJV), we too must remain focused on doing His will, lest we become distracted by any philosophy or deceit of the adversary to deprive us of the Father's promise. We must strive to be faithful even as Yeshua was faithful.

Evil spirits promoting doctrines of demons lurked behind teachers of the Gospel with naysayers, spies, and doctrinal heretics, through beguiling demonic persuasion with a pretense of holiness. They followed closely behind the heels of Paul to enslave the new Christians and to deny the efficacy of Christ Jesus's work on the cross. Those same fallen spirits continue to contest the truth of Yehovah's plan, purchase, and purpose of believers today. Satan and his minions did not know the effect of the crucifixion of the Savior until after He had been crucified, risen from the dead, and set at liberty those who had been held captive (Luke 4:18, 1 Pet. 3:19, Eph. 4:8).

> But this Man, after He had offered one sacrifice for sins
> forever, sat down at the right hand of God, from that time
> waiting till His enemies are made His footstool. (Heb.
> 10:12 NKJV)

> And they overcame him by the blood of the Lamb and by
> the word of their testimony, and they did not love their lives
> to the death. (Rev. 12:11 NKJV)

We continue to war against darkness not with weapons of men but with the weapons of the Spirit of God, His gifts and talents as distributed to each believer (Eph. 6:10–20).

The battle was on. Darkness must destroy what Yehovah had determined invincible. The Galatians had received salvation by faith and the power of the Holy Spirit, not by the works of the Law but by faith in their Messiah's atoning sacrifice. Paul was deeply troubled by the entrapments this heresy of legalism could cause; man could not be justified by the Mosaic Law, as the Law itself condemned all men. That was its intent, to expose man's propensity to sin, to compel mankind to seek redemption, to somehow be liberated from his pervasive sin nature through someone, for the Law came that sin might abound or *increase* (Rom. 5:20 ESV, Ezek. 20:25)! The Apostle Paul knew the power of the Holy Spirit would be stymied by those attempting to justify themselves by works of the Law (Gal. 3:2).

> Therefore He who supplies the Spirit to you and works
> miracles among you, does He do it by the works of the law,
> or by the hearing of faith? (Gal. 3:5 NKJV)

It is a simple and direct question whose answer is an unequivocal "hearing by faith." Recall that many of the Galatians had no previous Torah instruction, nor did they understand its many observances and commands. There apparently were Hebrews with a rudimentary understanding of the Torah, to whom Paul was referring, who he would encounter on occasion and who were promoting portions of the Torah (i.e., the Mosaic Covenant), which Paul was vigorously opposing as an obligation for the New Covenant believer. Herein lies the doctrinal confusion that persists to this day, a misguided resurgence to respect the Torah by observing some abstract of the Mosaic Covenant commands. What about the Ten Commandments? What about the Mosaic Covenant? Did it pass away? Do we observe the Sabbath Day or the Lord's Day? What part of the Old Testament should we now adhere, as we dare not to say, "Cast it off"?

Many Christians simply do not understand there is a legal conveyance from the Mosaic Law to the New Covenant that gives birth to Christian liberty (Luke 4:18). Others are misled, either purposefully or ignorantly, by denominational doctrine or errant theology as to what Mosaic Covenant rules and strictures they should continue to follow as it pertains to the Gentile believer. Many cults and some churches take wanton license with various scriptures, manipulating and coercing followers through deceit, controlling, and often "shepherding" the flock with mal intent, resulting in a duplicitous faith. Many of these organizations are nothing more than profit-seeking companies that use Mosaic Law as a fear tactic to extract tithes, offerings, inheritances, wills, and insurance policies from their attendees. Following flamboyant or charismatic religious leaders without a correct knowledge of Yeshua Hamashiach obscures Yehovah's unrelenting pursuit and passion for His children and diminishes true and unfettered worship, leading to spiritual blindness, confusion, and despair. Our adversaries are persistent, unrelenting, and diabolical in their pursuit of our deception and destruction. It is imperative that the Christian believer stay rooted in the grace afforded us in the Word of Yehovah and continually seek the counsel of the Holy Spirit for discernment and guidance. Taking the word of the preacher, prophet, or teacher without serious personal inquiry in study and prayer can be disastrous to the well-intentioned and unsuspecting. This warning from Hosea holds true for many today:

> My people are destroyed for lack of knowledge. Because you have rejected knowledge, I also will reject you from being priest for Me; Because you have forgotten the law of your God, I also will forget your children. (Hosea 4:6 NKJV)

That prophecy sounds harsh, but the people had already rejected Yehovah's counsel and law; there remained no other possible outcome. We, brothers and sisters, are exhorted to be vigilant and stand fast in our liberty (Gal. 5:1), as we are not ignorant of the enemies many vices.

Jesus said to the Jews,

> "You search the Scriptures, for in them you think you have eternal life; and these are they which testify of Me. But you are not willing to come to Me that you may have life." (John 5:39–40 NKJV)

How did the learned Jews know the scriptures so well and still miss the Messiah? Why were their eyes blinded to the one they were seeking for millennia? Jesus acknowledges their diligence in searching the scriptures, but somewhere along the line, they failed to see Him! Modern Christianity has done much the same in supplanting our liberty afforded us through the death of Jesus with a hybrid Torah-works-based theology that compels believers to accept erroneous teachings and observations of the Law of Moses, despite their teaching being contrary to the Law of the Spirit of Life. In Romans 8:2, we find the two spiritual laws.

> For the law of the Spirit of life in Christ Jesus has made me free from the law of sin and death. (Rom. 8:2 NKJV)

This is where we must be careful not to fall into yeast fellowship; wherein a little leaven leavens the whole loaf, a little works justification can ruin the entire basket of grace. The apostle Paul warned us not to attempt to be justified by the law:

> You have become estranged from Christ, you who attempt to be justified by law; you have fallen from grace. (Gal. 5:4 NKJV)

We need not alienate ourselves from the grace of God by abiding with some aspect of the Law; nor should we think that we cannot return to walking in His grace. We simply need to put our hope and trust in His New Covenant, as it is precisely why He has given it to us!

CHAPTER 5

THE PLAN OF YEHOVAH TRANSITIONED THROUGH MULTIPLE COVENANTS

The first promise Yehovah made to Abram is in Genesis 12:1–3:

> Now the Lord had said to Abram: "Get out of your country, from your family and from your father's house, to a land that I will show you. I will make you a great nation; I will bless you and make your name great; And you shall be a blessing. I will bless those who bless you, And I will curse him who curses you; And in you all the families of the earth shall be blessed." (Gen. 12:1–3 NKJV)

Father did not exclude the Gentile family from His plan; He made provision for us through Abram as well (Gal. 3:8).

In Genesis 15:17–21, Yehovah executes a covenant with Abram, a promise to him and his descendants:

> And it came to pass, when the sun went down and it was dark, that behold, there appeared a smoking oven and a

burning torch that passed between those pieces. On the same day, the Lord made a covenant with Abram, saying: "To your descendants I have given this land, from the river of Egypt to the great river, the river Euphrates—the Kenites, the Kenezzites, the Kadmonites, the Hittites, the Perizzites, the Rephaim, the Amorites, the Canaanites, the Girgashites, and the Jebusites." (Gen. 15:17–21 NKJV)

In Ezekiel 36:26–28, we have a glimpse of the promise of the Holy Spirit, who was to come after Pentecost, after the New Covenant is consummated. Ezekiel was already living under the Mosaic Covenant, and he is now speaking of a new heart and a new spirit:

"I will give you a new heart and put a new spirit within you; I will take the heart of stone out of your flesh and give you a heart of flesh. I will put My Spirit within you and cause you to walk in My statutes, and you will keep My judgments and do them. Then you shall dwell in the land that I gave to your fathers; you shall be My people, and I will be your God." (Ezek. 36:26–28 NKJV)

This prophecy is currently being fulfilled through the many Messianic Hebrews who witnessed and believed in Messiah's baptism into death, then resurrection into life, and who baptizes us as well, from death into life (John 1:33, Acts 2:1–4), for they certainly received the baptism in the Holy Spirit, though they do not yet possess the physical Promised Land in its entirety.

Some are confused by the various covenants, ancient prophecies, and laws in the Bible that existed before, during, and after the Mosaic Covenant—and understandably so. As we piece together the abstract plan of covenants, prophecies, and laws, we discover their relevance in the New Covenant. Sin has always been sin. It was present in heaven with Lucifer and the angels that fell, it was present in the Garden of Eden with Adam and the Fall of all mankind, and it existed through each Covenant that Yehovah has ordered with man. Sin is the crux of the matter. How the Father dealt with its effect on humanity through the ages as His plan transitioned from one dispensation and revelation to the next, through His covenants and promises with Adam, Noah, Abraham, Moses, David, and Christ Jesus; He slowly unveiled His path toward our redemption, purposefully and methodically, proclaiming and pointing the way to Yeshua Hamashiach. Observances changed with each proceeding covenant. Things that were once not specifically commanded or observed would later be required in the Mosaic Covenant sacrifices, feast and holy days, circumcision, Sabbath observances, and tithes. When the New Covenant was consummated, many of those observances were set aside; now satisfied in Christ Jesus, they could no longer continue. Paul addresses this head-on in the book of Hebrews, writing to those who understood the Mosaic Covenant (Levitical system):

> Therefore, if perfection were through the Levitical priesthood (for under it the people received the law), what further need was there that another priest should rise according to the order of Melchizedek, and not be called according to the order of Aaron? For the priesthood being changed, of necessity there is also a change of the law. (Heb. 7:11–12 NKJV)

Due to the increase of iniquity, Yehovah determined an intermediate covenant, the Mosaic Covenant (a.k.a. Aaronic or Levitical priesthood), which prophesied of the eternal Messiah and supplied a temporary covering of the sins of mankind in the meantime. This covenant required the blood of sacrificial animals until the promised Messiah should come, who would be the perfect, unblemished, holy sacrifice that Yehovah required to satisfy His wrath and justice. There was, however, a human problem. The Mosaic Covenant was wrought with human deficiency and sin. Yehovah needed a new priesthood and a New Covenant, for neither the Adamic blood line nor the Levitical priestly lineage of Aaron could ever produce a sinless soul that met the righteous requirement of the Mosaic Law. Father had to supply a sinless sacrifice, birthed of a holy Seed, one of eternal existence and one who would be grafted into the defiled lineage of Adam. Yehovah needed a perfect priest to be His sacrifice to atone for us. Subsequently, there was of necessity a change of the priesthood from the Aaronic line to Yeshua Hamashiach. There was also of necessity (Rom. 7:12) a change involving the Law of Moses! So what did it change to? Let us look at Hebrews 7:16:

> Who has come, not according to the law of a fleshly commandment. (Heb. 7:16a NKJV)

No longer in accordance with the Law of Moses but "according to the power of an endless life." That endless life is Yehovah incarnate, the Lord Yeshua Hamashiach, the only begotten Son of Yehovah, who created all things and who is the embodiment of holiness and righteousness. Our condition and position before Yehovah are no longer based on our performance or obedience to the Law but on the righteousness of Christ Jesus's endless life! Those who accept and believe in Christ Jesus's atoning sacrifice are hidden in Christ Jesus for eternity. They have become one with Him and the Father, perfected through His atoning sacrifice and kept in Him by the infilling and ever-present Holy Spirit.

Reading further, we again bump into another scripture clearly defining the ended state of the Mosaic Covenant:

> For on the one hand there is an annulling of the former commandment because of its weakness and unprofitableness, for the law made nothing perfect; on the other hand, there is the bringing in of a better hope, through which we draw near to God. (Heb. 7:18–19 NKJV)

A better covenant, established on better promises than had been given to Moses (Heb. 8:6), has been given to us, by which we desire more intimate fellowship with the Father. This is Hallelujah time! Clinging to the decaying vestiges of the Mosaic Covenant (Heb. 8:13), denying the propitiatory work of Yeshua, is not going to satisfy your desire for righteousness, and it will most certainly not please the Spirit of Grace.

> Having wiped out the handwriting of requirements that was against us, which was contrary to us. And He has taken it out of the way, having nailed it to the cross. (Col. 2:14 NKJV)

We find here that the binding observations and rites of cleanliness are satisfied in Christ Jesus's crucifixion. Many of the Mosaic observances were burdensome and unpleasant. Yehovah Himself had no pleasure in them, as is shown in Psalm 40:6 and Hebrews 10:6.

> Sacrifice and offering You did not desire; My ears You have opened. Burnt offering and sin offering You did not require. (Ps. 40:6 NKJV)

This is a prophecy of Yeshua Hamashiach's forthcoming sacrifice and His testament that Yehovah does not enjoy the bloodletting costs of covering man's sin, as stated in the phrase "Burnt offering and sin offering You did not require" (desired not, no pleasure in). Also, in Hebrews 10:6,

> In burnt offerings and sacrifices for sin You had no pleasure. (Heb. 10:6 NKJV)

Substitutionary sacrifices were needful as a temporary measure to appease Yehovah's righteous indignation and to keep mankind from destruction until a perfect sacrificial lamb, Yeshua Hamashiach, could come to satisfy the offense that kindled the Father's wrath. Yehovah has limits to His mercy, and He will not endure an unrepentant, recalcitrant mankind for eternity. Yehovah offers mankind the option to live according to His perfect nature, with the enablement of His own Holy Spirit, or to rebel and live one's own selfish desire. Rejecting His mercy toward us, as provisioned through His grace in Christ Jesus's atonement, leaves no avenue to His righteousness; damnation is the self-imposed curse of the self-willed soul.

Deceit abounds everywhere we look in this world. Satan has devolved into an immeasurable depth of depravity, with hostility toward all things righteous and holy. His fate having been sealed for eternal destruction, he still lurks as a roaring lion, seeking someone to devour through lies and deceit. His envy drives him to destroy the righteous works of Yehovah, to destroy Yehovah's creation and attempt an overthrow of the Father's good kingdom. The apostle Paul addresses Satan's tools of philosophy and deceit in Colossians 2:8, which will help us a great deal in understanding Colossians 2:14.

> Beware lest anyone cheat you through philosophy and empty deceit, according to the tradition of men, according to the basic principles of the world, and not according to Christ. (Col. 2:8 NKJV)

Recall that Paul's contention was against the law of circumcision, which seems a little out of place in our modern-day society, but it was an act of sanctification, a sign in the flesh of the Jew/Hebrew to set them apart from the Gentile and as a mark toward holiness and cleanliness. Circumcision, as we will come to see, plays a significant role in the identity of the Jewish nation and underpins their adamant adherence to its institution as a means of salvation. Circumcision sanctified the nation, per Yehovah's command. Its compliance was paramount to the Hebrew culture, heritage, and salvation. Moses was almost slain for not circumcising his son. Yehovah would raise up another leader to replace Moses if Zipporah, his wife, had not relented and circumcised their son (Exod. 4:24). Circumcision was the sign of the covenant that Yehovah made with Abraham for the Hebrew nation, and He would not deviate from it. When the apostle Paul began to preach the revelation of Christ' New Covenant, one final sacrifice for all sin for all time, to the exclusion of the Mosaic Law, there was great upheaval in Israel among the religious hypocrites. Yehovah had set in place a time of demarcation from the Law of Moses, to one of faith in Christ Jesus's "power of an endless life" atonement (Heb. 7:16 NKJV). A time to believe in His Son's sacrifice, as prophesied by the prophets, to trust in Yehovah's grace and mercy. Even as Yehovah provided extraordinary signs in the desert to the Jewish exiles, Jesus performed innumerable signs and wonders before the nation of Israel. Yehovah came to redeem those who would trust in His promises to Abraham and Moses, but it required faith in His plan of mercy and not on keeping of the Law. Many Hebrew children believed, and persecution flowed from the Jewish religious leaders. Others did not believe and rebelled against Yehovah and His gift, denying their Messiah and, with it, their own means of salvation.

As faith in Yehovah's promises to Abram is central to the Gentiles' belief in sanctification and salvation by faith, the children of Israel trusted in the sign of circumcision as one's testament of faith in Yehovah. Yehovah cojoined both the Gentile and the Messianic Hebrews under the patriarch

Abram/Abraham, the father of many nations, through two separate covenants—one by promise and one by circumcision (Gen. 12:1–4).

So when did circumcision become so vital to the Jew as instituted in the Law of Moses? Not until after Yehovah had made redemptive promises to Abram, 430 years before He instituted the practice of circumcision with Moses in the Sinaitic covenant. Yehovah made His promise to Abram when he was seventy-five years of age because Abram believed in Yehovah and chose not to serve the many idols that his father, Terah, had worshipped. This covenant of promise is important to the Gentile in that Abram was not a Hebrew or Jew but more akin to the Gentile when Yehovah made Abram the promise. Later, Abram goes to Egypt, returns to Canaan, is separated from Lot, rescues Lot, and then meets the priest Melchizedek, King of Salem, who also blesses Abram. Abram is not yet considered a Hebrew or Jew, as the twelve tribes of Israel—that is, Jacob's sons—did not exist until the seventy souls of Jacob's house departed Canaan and left for Egypt, approximately 190 years later. Even thereafter, Israel, the name given to the nation of Israel, could not exist until after their exodus from Egypt, as they were slaves in Egypt for centuries, prospering under barbaric conditions until their exodus. Not until the people arrived at Mt. Sinai could they be considered a legitimate nation, a people under common rule and covenant with Yehovah. Thus, Abram was a Gentile when he received his second promise from Melchizedek, one who is made like unto the Son of Yehovah, a priest who abides forever (Hebrews 7:3). Here, Melchizedek is representative of the coming Word of Yehovah, Immanuel, Yeshua Hamashiach, and he bestows a blessing upon Abram while he is still uncircumcised and therefore a Gentile. Thereafter, Abram laments that he has no son (Gen. 15:3), and Yehovah promises him so many sons that Abram could not count them. So where is the sign of circumcision? It still does not occur even when Abram, now aged eighty-six years, takes Sarai's maidservant, Hagar, to wife, and she bares him a son named Ishmael. However, he is not the son of promise. Then, thirteen years later, when Abram was ninety-nine, Yehovah made Abram another promise. Abraham received his son of the promise the following year when he was aged one hundred years, along with a sign of the covenant of promise, circumcision, and a name change to Abraham—father of many nations (Gen. 17:10–11). Yehovah required the sign of circumcision as an act to validate Abram's faith and to confirm Abram as the father of the Jewish nation that would follow him. This simple twenty-four year chronology establishes Abram as the father of the believing Gentiles as well as the father of the believing Jews.

Just as, "Abraham believed God, and it was accounted to him for righteousness" (Gen. 15:6, Rom. 4:3 NKJV).

> Therefore, know that only those who are of faith are sons of Abraham. And the Scripture, foreseeing that God would justify the Gentiles by faith, preached the gospel to Abraham beforehand, saying, "In you all the nations shall be blessed." So, then those who are of faith are blessed with believing Abraham. (Gal. 3:6–9 NKJV)

I love this scripture because it witnesses the forethought of God to justify and redeem the Gentile too, long before the Mosaic Covenant came along.

In support of both the promise to Abraham and the Mosaic Covenant, Jesus kept Himself under the Law of Moses, circumcised the eighth day after his birth. He would never violate its commands, and His teachings were always in keeping with it. He often rebuked the religious leaders for their treachery and abuse of the Law of Moses, as He likewise informed the scribes and Pharisees that they should have paid tithes, as they were under the Law (Matt. 23:23), without neglecting the weightier elements of the Law, such as justice, mercy, and faith. The apostle Paul addresses the giving issue on several occasions, as we will address later, but for now, just know that Yehovah does not judge His children according to the Law (Rom. 6:14b). You are free to honor Him and support the ministry of the Gospel as your heart desires.

> So let each one give as he purposes in his heart, not grudgingly or of necessity; for God loves a cheerful giver. (2 Cor. 9:7 NKJV)

In Paul's letter to Timothy, we read,

> Now the purpose of the commandment is love from a pure heart, from a good conscience, and from sincere faith, from

> which some, having strayed, have turned aside to idle talk,
> desiring to be teachers of the law, understanding neither
> what they say nor the things which they affirm. (1 Tim.
> 1:7 NKJV)

Or are we missing something more than just fiscal accountability here? Where else have we digressed in today's pulpits? Confusion abounds due to the import of legalism into the body of Christ and its endless demands for a works-based theology, yet many have little inclination as to its basis or its damaging effects. Many teachers continue to skew the requirements of righteousness, as though they could be attained by keeping the Ten Commandments, the basis for the whole of the Mosaic Law and its strictures, or by keeping the Sabbath, or paying tithes. So, why not circumcision, which symbolically is the foundational commandment of the Abrahamic Covenant, which denoted faith, sanctification, and purity? Christians should know that Christ Jesus set us free from the curse of the Law (Gal. 3:13) and that He has set us at liberty from the Law of Moses (2 Cor. 3:17); however, some are instructed to keep the law of the Sabbath and pay tithes, as they predate the Law of Moses and are assumed, therefore, still applicable. Though this is partly true, they do not mention that these were also performed prior to the Law of Moses outside of any commandment. The seventh day, when Yehovah rested, is in Genesis 2:3. The distinction between the prelaw and the lawful commandment is less clear when one considers that their observances are not known to have been instituted by commandment and the frequency of their observances is unknown. If all of Moses's ancestors, from Adam up until Moses, kept the Sabbath and paid tithes, a span of 2,500 years, there is no evidence or recording of them until Abram, and there is not one curse levied against any, as there was apparently no legally binding commandment to perform them. Nonetheless, they probably did honor the Sabbath and supported ministers of faith, such as Melchizedek, and others who were poor or in need, prior to the giving of the Law of Moses. The distinction is not whether they did or did not make observances but whether they were constrained by commandment. I believe both issues are addressed clearly in the New Covenant, being absorbed into the preeminent Law of Matthew 22:37–40.

Yehovah performed the first animal sacrifice in the Garden of Eden to cover the nakedness of Adam and Eve. Later, Abel prepared an animal for the Lord (Gen. 4:4) and was accepted, and a couple of thousand years later, Abraham performed a sacrifice when receiving the covenant promise from Yehovah (Gen. 15:17–18). Abram also gave a tithe as a freewill honorarium to Melchizedek, a type of Christ Jesus, and not by a requirement of the Mosaic Law, which did not yet exist. There was no commandment to observe the Sabbath in Genesis 2:3, though Yehovah sanctified and called it holy; we must conclude that that is reason enough. Still, there was no explicit instruction given to Adam to observe the Sabbath, maybe because the Tree of Knowledge of Good and Evil already determined the fallen state of man, and adding more disobedience to the legend of offenses would have been superfluous. Neither Seth, Noah, nor Abraham or any of the forefathers are known to have been instructed to keep the Sabbath Day's rest or to perform animal sacrifices, though Abel did present a lamb offering to Yehovah (Gen. 4:2), as did Noah in Genesis 8:20. We must conclude that it was known, customary, and pleasing to Yehovah.

The act of the tithe and the act of circumcision are not made clear in the canonized text until Abram. Nonetheless, these actions would have been acceptable, given their adherence to the first and greatest commandment that existed long before the Mosaic Covenant, undoubtedly through eternity past. Jesus tells us what that first and great commandment is in Matthew 22:36–40:

> "Teacher, which is the great commandment in the law?" Jesus said to him, "'You shall love the Lord your God with all your heart, with all your soul, and with all your mind.' This is the first and great commandment. And the second is like it: 'You shall love your neighbor as yourself.' On these two commandments hang all the Law and the Prophets." (Matt. 22:36–40 NKJV)

It remains that all later commandments must be inferior to the first and great commandment but also be in support of it. The Law of Moses was given as a servant to this greater commandment and its purpose.

> For who has known the mind of the Lord? Or who has
> become His counselor? (Rom. 11:34 NKJV)

The heavens declare the glory of Yehovah (Ps. 19:1), and the angels sing his praises, crying "Holy, holy, holy!" To love Him is not a duty but an honor and privilege to worship. Adam experienced the glory of Yehovah before the Fall and assuredly witnessed his experience to his children and great-great-grandchildren. The awesomeness of Yehovah is beyond our comprehension today; understandably, we struggle to grasp how great He truly is. Sufficient for today is our trouble, but one day soon, we will see Him again, face-to-face, even as Adam did. Until then, we see Him in the person of our Lord Yeshua Hamashiach, the manifest glory of Yehovah, who came and dwelt among man to heal, deliver, and set captives free.

Those who believe in Christ Jesus have been perfected forever by one sacrifice (Heb. 10:12,14) and not by any work, nor by the Law of Moses, and certainly not by circumcision or the tithe.

Mosaic observances and countless more "laws of the Jews" caused the sheep to lose sight of their true redemption in Christ. As grievous as these actions are, they are superficial in comparison to the spiritual damage sown across the souls of Yehovah's children whose faith has been altered to trust in justification by works, to appease the preacher or denominational creed more than the working of their faith in the atoning sacrifice of the Lord Yeshua Hamashiach! These tactics discourage believers, deceiving them that Yehovah is unsatisfied and angry and that they do not measure up to implied demands. They have been deceived to trust in works of the flesh to secure deliverance by some of the very tenets that were originally imposed by the Law of Moses to guarantee failure.

> Therefore I also gave them up to statutes that were not
> good, and judgments by which they could not live. (Ezek.
> 20:25 NKJV)

Believers who desire an intimate relationship with the Father are often frustrated and discouraged from doing so, having an aura of insignificance and failure, a lingering doubt of the Father's acceptance. These feelings of inadequacy are the result of the browbeating they receive from errant teachers intermingling the curse of the Law and man-made laws into the gospel of grace. Satan is a deceitful manipulator, as he questioned God's instruction to Adam and Eve: "And he said unto the woman, yeah, hath God said?" (Gen. 3:1 KJV). The mere suggestion of deniability becomes the wedge to split trust away from the child of God. We cannot allow our affection and hope to be derailed by menacing half-truths. We have a promise and an everlasting hope in the work of the Lord Jesus that redeems us from the curse of the Law.

> For the law of the Spirit of life in Christ Jesus has made me free from the law of sin and death. For what the law could not do in that it was weak through the flesh, Yehovah did by sending His own Son in the likeness of sinful flesh, on account of sin: He condemned sin in the flesh, that the righteous requirement of the law might be fulfilled in us who do not walk according to the flesh but according to the Spirit. (Rom. 8:2–4 NKJV)

We cannot drink from the same fountain both bitter and sweet water; that, my friends, is the wrong fountain. Some have poisoned the fountain, and the child of God must discern the truth in the Word of God.

We must choose to enter His presence with a thankful heart, a clean conscience, and freedom from bondage to the Mosaic Covenant and its authority to impute sin.

> Having wiped out the handwriting of requirements that was against us, which was contrary to us. And He has taken it out of the way, having nailed it to the cross. (Col. 2:14 NKJV)

All the Levitical rites, commandments, and religious duties have been nailed to His cross! We are at liberty to enjoy true worship with unbounded thanksgiving and freedom to love without condemnation! No longer are holy days, Sabbath days, feast days, new moons, tithes, circumcision, and animal sacrifices required for your justification. This, too, is the Good News, the Gospel of Yeshua Hamashiach!

Note Peter's warning against circumcision and the keeping of the Law:

> Now therefore why tempt ye God, to put a yoke upon the
> neck of the disciples, which neither our fathers nor we were
> able to bear? (Acts 15:10 NKJV)

Firstly, why tempt ye Yehovah? Not only can you not keep the Law, but trying to do so, even to suggest such a thing, is an affront to Yehovah. He knows you cannot do it, so do not make Him to be a liar, nor try to convince yourself that you could. That is dangerous territory. Neither they nor their forefathers kept the Law, and neither can we today. Beware of the yoke binders, those who desire to control your devotion with the rod of legalism, exalting themselves above the Lord's marvelous grace!

We have neglected the purpose for which Yehovah made a New Covenant and have insulted the Spirit of Grace by reinserting Mosaic commands and its legal tenets back onto the body of Christ. It was for freedom that Christ set us free:

> Stand fast therefore in the liberty by which Christ has
> made us free, and do not be entangled again with a yoke of
> bondage. (Gal. 5:1 NKJV)

That liberty would be freedom from all aspects of the Mosaic Law and its power to impute sin and condemnation upon us. We have been set free by "the power of an endless life" (Heb. 7:16 NKJV) Again, in Hebrews 7:19 (NKJV), "for the law made nothing perfect." We now have a better hope, by which we can draw nigh unto Yehovah and enjoy His fellowship as sons and daughters (Heb. 7:19b).

> For you, brethren, have been called to liberty; only do not
> use liberty as an opportunity for the flesh, but through love
> serve one another. (Gal. 5:13 NKJV)

Liberty is not freedom to do iniquity but the power to overcome evil with good. It does not free us from temptation, but it grants us the power to overcome temptation. It denies sin's hold on us and gives us the power to choose and to do better, to follow the leading of the Holy Spirit and change our character from who we were before to the child Yehovah desires and delights in.

> In Him you were also circumcised with the circumcision made without hands, by putting off the body of the sins of the flesh, by the circumcision of Christ, buried with Him in baptism, in which you also were raised with Him through faith in the working of Yehovah, who raised Him from the dead. (Col. 2:11–12 NKJV)

The new circumcision is not the cutting of flesh but the putting off the sins of the flesh, to overcome them and render its power void. Liberty is for well doing, to grow in the grace of Yeshua Hamashiach to become vibrant, joyous, merciful, and good, even as He is.

CHAPTER 6

THE ABRAHAMIC AND MOSAIC COVENANTS

Let us look at Abraham, a fellow sojourner, a wanderer in the Promised Land. Abraham's journey is an analogy for seeking an eternal habitation with the Father. Our wanderlust will never be satisfied here on this earth. We, too, long for and look forward to Yehovah's eternal home. Abram's search brought him to consider the existence and acceptance of the one true God (Gal. 3:6–9 NKJV), just as Abraham "believed God, and it was accounted to him for righteousness." Therefore, know that only those who are of faith are sons of Abraham. And the scripture, foreseeing that God would justify the Gentiles by faith, preached the gospel to Abraham beforehand, saying, "In you all the nations shall be blessed." So then those who are of faith are blessed with believing Abraham.

Our acceptance of the eternal Creator remains the qualifier for us today.

> But without faith it is impossible to please Him, for he who comes to God must believe that He is, and that He is a rewarder of those who diligently seek Him. (Heb. 7:6 NKJV)

Yehovah included His love for the Gentiles within this same covenant. He did not forget about us. He made provision for all flesh to be saved but only at the proper time and through the proper Seed. There was a plan, and it would take some time before the appointed Savior appeared.

As it was for Abraham, so too was it for the Hebrew and the Gentile; "only those who are of faith are sons of Abraham" (Gal. 3:9 NKJV). Yehovah did not justify the Hebrew or the Gentile by any work of the Mosaic Law; He justifies us through faith in His Son's atoning sacrifice (John 3:14–16), the promised Seed to come, whose blood cleanses us from all sin and imputes His righteousness into us. By faith, we trust and accept the Father's promise, just as Abraham did, through His Son, Christ Jesus, the King David "type" prophesied in Ezekiel 37:24–25.

Yehovah gave the Law to Moses and to the children of Israel in Exodus 16:23–30. He gave them the Sabbath rest as a solemn rest, a holy Sabbath unto the Lord. It is important to see that Yehovah did not give the Sabbath commandment to the Gentile, nor to Abraham or any of his predecessors. The Law of Moses, or Mosaic Covenant, was intended solely for the then-present Hebrew children, not for their forefathers.

> The Lord our God made a covenant with us in Horeb. The Lord did not make this covenant with our fathers, but with us, those who are here today, all of us who are alive. (Deut. 5:2–3 NKJV)

It is quite clear that Adam, Noah, Abraham, and all those in between were not given this covenant and therefore were not under any obligation to observe it.

Next, we see that there are grave difficulties with trying to live the perfect life in accordance with the Law of Moses, which is embodied in the Torah. The Mosaic Covenant was perfect and without flaw. It came straight from Yehovah. Trying to keep it, however, was man's undoing. He needed the Holy Spirit's help to keep even one commandment of Yehovah, but the Holy Spirit had not yet been poured out.

> "And I gave them My statutes and showed them My judgments, which, if a man does, he shall live by them." (Ezek. 20:11 NKJV)

> "Yet the house of Israel rebelled against Me in the wilderness; they did not walk in My statutes; they despised My judgments." (Ezek. 20:13 NKJV)

> "Because they despised My judgments and did not walk in My statutes, but profaned My Sabbaths; for their heart went after their idols." (Ezek. 20:16 NKJV)

> "Therefore I also gave them up to statutes that were not good, and judgments by which they could not live." (Ezek. 20:25 NKJV)

Have you ever neglected any of Yehovah's judgments or ever fallen short of perfection? Of course, you have. We still fail today; even with the New Covenant and the abiding Holy Spirit, we stumble when we concern ourselves with matters of this world and our fleshly indulgences. We must walk the path of sanctification in this life, laying aside those things that so easily ensnare us (Heb. 12:1). I am very thankful that our Father extends His mercy toward us:

> For by grace you have been saved through faith, and that not of yourselves; it is the gift of God, not of works, lest anyone should boast. (Eph. 2:8 NKJV)

> For as many as are of the works of the law are under the curse; for it is written, "Cursed is everyone who does not continue in all things which are written in the book of the law, to do them." But that no one is justified by the law in the sight of God is evident, for "the just shall live by faith." Yet the law is not of faith, but "the man who does them shall live by them. Christ has redeemed us from the curse of the law, having become a curse for us (for it is written, cursed is everyone who hangs on a tree"), that the blessing of Abraham might come upon the Gentiles in Christ Jesus, that we might receive the promise of the Spirit through faith. (Gal. 3:10–14 NKJV)

Here is a startling revelation (Gal. 3:12 NKJV): "the man who does them shall live by them." Keeping the Law was not an act of faith; it was an act of compliance. He must live by them. There was no faith expended to trust the efficacy of the Law to redeem them by grace; it was a faith built entirely contingent upon their obedience. The diligence needed to adhere to its many strict commands weighed upon the follower, who would recall the terror they experienced at the foot of Mt. Sinai, so much so that they begged to hear no more of it. The Law demanded perfection by its tenets, which in turn imperiled the follower by its curses. Hence, their works could not save them, and no man could be justified by the Law, as none could keep it. Lawful compliance depended on the diligent compliance of man, a repetitive failure, and not on Yehovah's grace.

So what is the answer? What is the work that the Christian believer must now do since he cannot acquire salvation through keeping the Law?

We find the answer in John 6:29:

> Jesus answered and said to them, "This is the work of God, that you believe in Him whom He sent." (John 6:29 NKJV)

This simple instruction is multifaceted in that there is much more to believing in Christ as the Messiah, our Redeemer, and Son of Yehovah; we must accept His salvation based on His terms embodied in the New (Abrahamic) Covenant so that, by faith (Eph. 2:8), we acknowledge His sovereignty and grace to save us by His loving-kindness through His Promise.

Abraham's faith rested in a better covenant.

> But now He has obtained a more excellent ministry, inasmuch as He is also Mediator of a better covenant, which was established on better promises. (Heb. 8:6 NKJV)

> Brethren, I speak in the manner of men: Though it is only a man's covenant, yet if it is confirmed, no one annuls or adds to it. Now to Abraham and his Seed were the promises

made. He does not say, "And to seeds," as of many, but as of one, "And to your Seed," who is Christ. (Gal. 3:15–16 NKJV)

Jesus confirmed the promises of Yehovah to Abraham at Calvary by being the greater testator and High Priest who died!

Going back to God's promise in Genesis 12:1+, notice who is doing the covenant promising here. It is not Abraham; it is Yehovah! Abraham could not do anything to warrant or ensure his part of the covenant anyway. All he could do was trust that Yehovah was faithful and merciful and that Yehovah would complete what He had promised. Not only was Yehovah's promise to Abram, but it also held His promises of redemption He made to Adam, Noah, Enoch, Seth and the hosts of mankind to follow, most importantly to His own Son. Not much has changed over the millennia. We still cannot do anything to ensure our part of the covenant except to trust in the Father's promise. He does the work, He keeps His promises, and He keeps us!

The Mosaic Law was added 430 years later, like a late-coming addendum to the Abrahamic Covenant, though explicitly for the Hebrew children, as Yehovah's promise to Abram had already prefigured in the Gentiles' salvation plan. The Mosaic Covenant served not only as a vessel for the Seed to come but also as a tutor, a guide, and a teacher to define and expose all mankind's desperate enslavement to sin and eventually point us to a Savior who would deliver us, aside from our feeble noncompliance. See Galatians 3:19 for the Law's purpose.

It is important to not underestimate the preposition *till* or *until*. Firstly, it denotes the appointed period established by Yehovah the Father that the Covenant of Promise, the New Covenant was to be initiated. The promise was made not only to Abraham but also to Christ Jesus, the Seed to whom the promise was also made! It further identifies the end of the Law by the phrase "till the Seed should come" (Gal. 3:20 NKJV). So when the Seed comes, there is a setting aside of the old that the New Covenant may come (Hebrews 10:9).

Therefore, the law was our tutor to bring us to Christ, that we might be justified by faith. But after faith has come, we are no longer under a tutor. (Gal. 3:24 NKJV)

This promise, as later revealed, references our purpose (Eph. 2:5–7 NKJV)—we are Christ Jesus's inheritance—and provides understanding of the term *the body of Christ* as being in Christ, His body. We who believe in Him become one with Him, hidden in Him (Col. 3:3 NKJV), spiritual stones (1 Pet. 2:5 NKJV) being made to conform to His character and likeness. Herein lies the authority of Yeshua Hamashiach and the efficacy of His holy blood to cleanse and make whole those who trust in Him. Christ's blood redeems us back into His holiness so we can dwell in the presence of the Father with a pure conscience, without guilt or stain (Heb. 9:14 NKJV).

However precious His goodness is toward us we believe, Jesus sees His reward as far exceeding our own, for Paul says,

> Who for the joy set before Him endured the cross. (Heb. 12:2 NKJV)

> That you may know what is the hope of His calling, what are the riches of the glory of His inheritance in the saints, and what is the exceeding greatness of His power toward us who believe, according to the working of His mighty power. (Eph. 1:18–19 NKJV)

These are not idle statements of sympathy but are of the heartfelt passion of a Father who had lost His wayward prodigals and is now receiving them home! Our Father loves us beyond comprehension, and I, for one, am ecstatic about seeing Him in the fullness of His glory!

Secondly, it declares the coming end of the Mosaic Covenant. This statement may be objectionable to some; however, scripture is clear that the Mosaic Covenant could not save and must be replaced by a better covenant.

> Therefore, if perfection were through the Levitical priesthood (for under it the people received the law), what further need was there that another priest should rise according to the order of Melchizedek, and not be called according to the order of Aaron? For the priesthood being changed, of necessity there is also a change of the law. (Heb. 7:11–12 NKJV)

Jesus tells us directly when the Law and the prophets' dispensation would end for those held under the Mosaic Covenant, aside from the Abrahamic Covenant:

> The law and the prophets were until John. (Luke 16:16 NKJV)

Their tenure was coming to an end; thereafter, Jesus began preaching the kingdom of Yehovah. Then Jesus makes a peculiar statement:

> And it is easier for heaven and earth to pass away than for one tittle of the law to fail. (Luke 16:17 NKJV)

He knew what was to become of the Law of Moses and the power of Yehovah, who sustained its authority. Yehovah would not allow one stroke or tittle of the Law to fail. Jesus was going to keep every word and tittle to its fullest measure (Luke 24:44, Acts 13:29). The Law of Moses was designed to usher in the Messiah, and only by His own hand, with great difficulty, would the Law be set aside.

We find that the promised Seed's crucifixion encompasses and made obsolete the Old Covenant.

> In that He says, "A New Covenant," He has made the first obsolete. Now what is becoming obsolete and growing old is ready to vanish away. (Heb. 8:13 NKJV)

This prophecy is in reference to what was spoken in Jeremiah 31:31–32:

> "Behold, the days are coming, says the Lord, when I will make a New Covenant with the house of Israel and with the house of Judah—not according to the covenant that I made with their fathers in the day that I took them by the hand to lead them out of the land of Egypt, My covenant which they broke." (Jer. 31:31–32 NKJV)

Jeremiah confirmed the Old Covenant was made with their fathers and the fading away or vanishing of the first covenant; it was now passing away in Christ Jesus. Whereas "He has made the first obsolete" (Heb. 8:13 NKJV) clearly defines that the first covenant is vanishing. Strong's renders the word *obsolete* as "old, worn out" (G3822).

The prophet Jeremiah spoke of a time when the ark of the covenant would no longer be regarded. He foresaw its end for usefulness:

> "Then it shall come to pass, when you are multiplied and increased in the land in those days," says the Lord, "that they will say no more, 'The ark of the covenant of the Lord.' It shall not come to mind, nor shall they remember it, nor shall they visit it, nor shall it be made anymore." (Jer. 3:16–17 NKJV)

> Ordinances imposed until the time of redemption. (Heb. 9:10 NKJV)

That is, those ordinances imposed in the Book of the Law until Christ Jesus's atonement and consummation of the New Covenant. The ordinances ceased at the point of Christ's atoning sacrifice, our redemption.

> He takes away the first that He may establish the second. (Heb. 10:9 NKJV)

Christ took the Law away when He fulfilled it, and He proclaimed, "It is finished," for the New Covenant to come into force.

> For by one offering He has perfected forever those who are being sanctified. (Heb. 10:14 NKJV)

This scripture confirms the elimination of continuous sacrifices as performed under the Law for justification and redemption. No further sacrifice is needful or sufficient.

> Having wiped out the handwriting of requirements that
> was against us, which was contrary to us. And He has
> taken it out of the way, having nailed it to the cross. (Col.
> 2:14 NKJV)

This is a clear reference to the handwritten Book of the Law and its requirements being contrary to our sinful nature. The Law was perfect; man was not and could not attain to its holiness. Jesus nailed it to His cross and canceled its application forthwith to those who believe in Him (Gal. 3:11–14).

You may ask, "What about the Hebrew who was under the Law but does not believe in Messiah?" We find that their disposition does not change:

> For as many as have sinned without law will also perish
> without law, and as many as have sinned in the law will be
> judged by the law (for not the hearers of the law are just
> in the sight of Yehovah, but the doers of the law will be
> justified. (Rom. 2:12–13 NKJV)

Those who were never under the Law will be judged according to their own convictions (v. 14–15), and those who were under the Law of Moses but did not accept their Messiah and His blood atonement will be judged in accordance with the Law of Moses.

Christ Jesus has redeemed those who accept Him from the curse of the Law.

CHAPTER 7

SOMEONE HAD TO DIE

Not to discourage you from reading this chapter but its title pains me to know that my transgressions implored Christ Jesus to die for me, for us. Although I, we, will be eternally grateful for His sacrifice, mercy and grace, my only recourse is to love Him more.

> For the life of the flesh is in the blood, and I have given it to you upon the altar to make atonement for your souls; for it is the blood that makes atonement for the soul. (Lev. 17:11 NKJV)

Maybe we should have started with this scripture as it entails not only how the body is nourished but how it contains the power to sustain life. As we reflect on the Spirit of Life, and how it was the blood of Yeshua that was spilt; that death, while bruising the body could not extinguish the resurrection power that sustained it, the Spirit's presence contained within that life giving blood. Indeed, there is power in the blood, it is the Holy Spirit's communion!

> And for this reason He is the Mediator of the New Covenant, by means of death, for the redemption of the transgressions under the first covenant, that those who are called may receive the promise of the eternal inheritance. For where there is a testament, there must also of necessity

be the death of the testator. For a testament is in force after
men are dead, since it has no power at all while the testator
lives. (Heb. 9:15–16 NKJV)

The death of Abraham did not consummate the Promise, his death
did nothing regarding the promise that Yehovah had made to Abraham
and to his descendants. Abraham did not resurrect; he had no power to do
so. Here, Yehovah the Father makes a promise to Himself, as embodied in
Christ the Son. Yehovah's Word made flesh, died on the cross for the sake
of the creation He loved. Now that the testator has died, the New Covenant
of promise is sealed and the Old Covenant was fulfilled and set aside, its use
now complete, there will be no more suitable sacrifices for sin.

Is the law then against the promises of God? Certainly not!
For if there had been a law given which could have given
life, truly righteousness would have been by the law. (Gal.
3:21 NKJV)

It is not possible for righteousness to be obtained by natural man
through the law. Adam did not obey one simple law and it brought about
all the sin, degradation, and death since that time upon all man and beast;
even the earth shakes beneath the iniquity of man, Gen. 2:17 (NKJV) "but
of the tree of the knowledge of good and evil you shall not eat, for in the day
that you eat of it you shall surely die." If it had been you or I, we certainly
would have fared no better than Adam. The Law, though intended to bring
life, brought the sting of death. The Law was not over-ruled or dismissed
but integrated into the plan, purchase, and purpose of Yehovah.

But the Scripture has confined all under sin that the
promise by faith in Jesus Christ might be given to those
who believe. But before faith came, we were kept under
guard by the law, kept for the faith which would afterward
be revealed. Therefore, the law was our tutor to bring us to
Christ, that we might be justified by faith. But after faith
has come, we are no longer under a tutor. (Gal. 3:22–25
NKJV)

The purpose of the Law was completed for both the Hebrew and for those who live by faith in Christ Jesus atoning sacrifice, that we might learn from it. Though the law was a tutor for both covenant types, those of faith in Yeshua are released from its implications'. We are now under the New Covenant, and whose Comforter is the Holy Spirit, who leads and guides us into all truth. The Old Covenant has been superseded. The New Covenant embraces all that the Old Covenant prepared us for, yet without the stringent Mosaic commands. Indeed, our new yoke is easy, and our burden is light. See Gal. 5:14 (NKJV)

> For all the law is fulfilled in one word, even in this: "You shall love your neighbor as yourself." (Matt. 22:37–38)

For those who continue to strive to live under the Law, there are obstacles. Yehovah forever ended the sacrifices of bulls and goats for the covering of the sins of man when the New Covenant was consummated at the death of Christ. For when the earthquake split the rocks, it also devastated the earthly Holy of Holies in the temple. The temple veil was torn when its supporting lintel stone collapsed, exposing the Holy of Holies, in which only the High Priest could enter once a year to make atonement for the sins of the nation. Yehovah was closing the Levitical priesthood system down, there would be no more annual sacrifice for the nation. Yeshua Hamashiach's death ended the Old Covenant while simultaneously consecrating the New Covenant in His blood. Yehovah caused the earthquake; it was an intentional declaration. He alone destroyed the stone temple on earth. Unlike previous destructions of the temple by opposing armies, this destruction was divinely appointed, and no man could contest its destroyer. He did it intentionally, proclaiming the consummation of His promise to Abraham (Hebrews 9:16), satisfying the Mosaic Law as the Holy Blood of the Messiah was sprinkled upon the true spiritual temple in heaven before the Father (Hebrews 9:12). One generation later, 40 years, the same amount of time allotted for the repentance of the Hebrew children in the desert, the destruction of the stone temple was completed by Titus in 70 AD. The temples destruction fulfilled Christ's prophecy that not one stone would be left upon another. Christ's sacrifice eliminated the role of the earthly High Priest and the sacrifices of bulls and goats for the atonement of sin. The perfect sacrifice of Christ's flesh and blood had finally been offered, no more shall there be need for another atoning sacrifice (Hebrews 10:12).

The Bondwoman and the Free Woman

Tell me, you who desire to be under the law, do you not hear the law? For it is written that Abraham had two sons: the one by a bondwoman, the other by a freewoman. But he who was of the bondwoman was born according to the flesh, and he of the freewoman through promise, which things are symbolic. For these are the two covenants: the one from Mount Sinai which gives birth to bondage, which is Hagar—for this Hagar is Mount Sinai in Arabia, and corresponds to Jerusalem which now is, and is in bondage with her children—but the Jerusalem above is free, which is the mother of us all. (Gal. 4: 21–26 NKJV)

There is a distinction being made between these two covenants, just as there is a distinction between the Mosaic Covenant, or First Covenant, as referred to by the Apostle Paul in Hebrews 8:7 NKJV, and the New Covenant. Mount Sinai in modern day Saudi Arabia is the esteemed mountain of Moses and the Ten Commandments. Unfortunately, it has been exalted, nearly idolized in modern Christianity that it shades the importance of the heavenly Jerusalem and by inference, the New Covenant along with its liberty. Mt. Sinai, read as the Mosaic Covenant, was of the slave woman, one held in bondage and servitude. Her predominance (the Mosaic Law) is extolled today that many Christians remain fixated on its commands and the earthly temple dwelling in Jerusalem that no longer exists, yet it gives birth to bondage (Hagar - Mt. Sinai - Jerusalem). This does not diminish the Old Covenants importance, nor the lessons which it teaches, however, the path to righteousness cannot be attained through it by fallen man.

The Mosaic Law is often skewed to manipulate and constrain believers with a spirit of fear, condemnation, and inadequacy. Though some aspects like circumcision and sacrifices are readily set aside, other tenets, such as keeping Torah (a contemporary euphemism for keeping the Law), observing the Sabbath, honoring the Lord's Day, Easter, Christmas, Good Friday,

Jewish holy days, paying tithes, mandatory fast days, lent, etc., are still employed. Some of these items are man-made and heretical, some can be observed without fear of bondage, while others should only be done in moderation for educational or historical relevance. When rites become dogma, the Gospel of Christ, the Good News, becomes obscured and even unrecognizable. There is as much power grabbing, pomp, greed, and pride in the pulpit as there is in Hollywood and the corporate boardroom. Mt. Sinai represents the bondage of the Mosaic Covenant and earthly Jerusalem; reverting to its structure and service is contrary to where the Holy Spirit is leading the Body of Christ. Sadly, many churches refuse to acknowledge the Mosaic Covenants obsolescence, its time of fulfillment and replacement, choosing to keep their assemblies in bondage to variations of Old Testament law; the very legal tenets Paul is refuting and for which all the apostles died preaching.

> But he who was of the bondwoman was born according to the flesh, and he of the freewoman through promise, which things are symbolic. For these are the two covenants: the one from Mount Sinai which gives birth to bondage, which is Hagar—for this Hagar is Mount Sinai in Arabia, and corresponds to Jerusalem which now is, and is in bondage with her children—but the Jerusalem above is free, which is the mother of us all. (Gal. 4:23–26 NKJV)

If you have seen the movie by Cecil B. DeMille, 'The Ten Commandments', you may recall the Mt. Sinai scene where Moses is summoned by Yehovah amidst the tumultuous wind, clouds, and fire. It is a very stirring and memorable scene. We have ascribed that same notion of awe and reverence to the Decalogue (Ten Commandments) as being the preeminent authority of all scripture; however, this is not the case. Mt. Sinai is extolled as being the holy place, a reverential mountain and was for blessing the people of Israel. Undoubtedly it was a blessing, until it was not kept; then the curses associated with that covenant proved to be catastrophic when if even one offense was committed, it often ended in death. Whether by an animal touching the mountain or a human transgression, disobedience had a severe outcome. In retrospect, the Children of Israel might have opted out of the Law given to Moses and awaited until a more favorable covenant was available, but there was no other option permitted and none could dare oppose the fiery, quaking mountain. They were imprisoned by their own transgressions, their idolatrous worship in Egypt and their exodus from Egypt to a barren land whose mountain smoked with fury. We are still of the same human makeup today as those standing at the foot of Mt. Sinai, I dare say our performance has been no greater than theirs. The Mt. Sinai covenant was the difference maker in their relationship with God. He, Yehovah used them as a steppingstone to bring about a temporary covenant, to provide an eternal sacrifice which was embedded in the Mosaic Covenant. Unfortunately, we have esteemed the Law given to Moses, as being greater than the spoken words of Jesus himself. Even as the Hebrew nation quivered because of their guilt-ridden sin, we will examine the correlation of those who refused to enter the Promised Land with those who at the present time refuse to enter the rest of Christ Jesus by not setting aside the Law of Moses; even as Christ did. (Hebrews 10:9) Jesus satisfied Yehovah's wrath that was stored up for us through the Fall of Adam and the Law of Moses. The unbelieving, that is, those who choose to remain in bondage to the Mosaic Law or any justification by works related law, deny the authority of Christ' work, and similarly deny themselves entry into the Lord's Sabbath Rest.

> "Take My yoke upon you and learn from Me, for I am gentle and lowly in heart, and you will find rest for your souls. For My yoke is easy and My burden is light." (Matt. 11:29–30 NKJV)

Yeshua Hamashiach is the liberator of our souls. His New Covenant yoke releases us from legal tenets so that we may rest in Him, our eternal Sabbath Days rest.

> Nevertheless what does the Scripture say? "Cast out the bondwoman and her son, for the son of the bondwoman shall not be heir with the son of the freewoman." So then, brethren, we are not children of the bondwoman but of the free. (Gal. 4:30–31 NKJV)

Plainly stated, the Law of Moses follower is to be cast out! Those who have regard to Mt. Sinai, the Mosaic Covenant, or earthly Jerusalem, cannot be heirs of the promise that Yehovah made to Abraham as it was made with respect to Abraham's faith that Yehovah was good, that He loved him, that He was trustworthy in providing a holy sacrifice in the coming Messiah. His faith, like Enoch's faith, was grounded in Yehovah's goodness,

> But without faith it is impossible to please Him, for he who comes to God must believe that He is, and that He is a rewarder of those who diligently seek Him. (Heb. 11:6 NKJV)

The works-oriented Law of Moses was built on the faithfulness of Yehovah but also on man to keep compliance with its laws. At their core, the Mosaic Law and the New Covenant are incongruent covenants, juxtaposed as it were to oppose one against the other, which simply cannot coexist in faith simultaneously. However, they are both Holy and perfect. The New Covenant of Grace excels in revealing Yehovah's grace to us; He knew we needed limitless grace.

> Indeed I, Paul, say to you that if you become circumcised, Christ will profit you nothing. And I testify again to every man who becomes circumcised that he is a debtor to keep the whole law. You have become estranged from Christ, you who attempt to be justified by law; you have fallen from grace. (Gal. 5:2–4 NKJV)

Here is the danger that Paul was concerned about, Christians falling from living in the grace of Yehovah afforded them by the one-time sacrifice of His Son Yeshua Hamashiach. Whether the lawful act was circumcision, observance of holy days, sanitary and dietary laws, tithing, or any other, they will not justify you before Yehovah because they are works based (Rom. 3:20, Gal. 2:16). You may elect to do or not to do them, howbeit; they must be done without compulsion, condemnation, or self-justification. The Blood of Christ Jesus is the only acceptable atonement for your salvation. Placing your trust in any other work effectively cuts you off from the profit of Christ' sacrifice.

> For the promise that he would be the heir of the world was
> not to Abraham or to his seed through the law, but through
> the righteousness of faith. (Rom. 4:13 NKJV)

It is not as though the Galatian Christians could not repent and cast off their works-based justification, circumcision in this case, and return to trusting in Messiah's atonement, but would they? We love to justify ourselves to prove our worth or opinion by performance, charity, persuasive speech, and a host of other works-oriented tasks. We are stubborn, mule-headed people and like to push the boundaries of our state in life, usually resulting in failure unless we repent. The pride of man is his own un-doing and is precisely the opposite of the humble spirit that Christ desires.

> For you, brethren, have been called to liberty; only do not
> use liberty as an opportunity for the flesh, but through love
> serve one another. (Gal. 5:13 NKJV)

True unfettered worship and devotion cannot be elicited by command or by keeping the works of the Law, coercion does not produce love, as proven by the religious hypocrites and even Paul himself prior to his conversion. Rather, there is a New Covenant directive on how we should serve one another,

> For all the law is fulfilled in one word, even in this: "You
> shall love your neighbor as yourself." (Gal. 5:14 NKJV)

> Jesus said to him, "'You shall love the Lord your God with
> all your heart, with all your soul, and with all your mind.'
> This is the first and great commandment. And the second
> is like it: 'You shall love your neighbor as yourself.' On these
> two commandments hang all the Law and the Prophets."
> (Matt. 22:37–40 NKJV)

Recall the woman condemned by the Pharisee as a sinner who anointed Jesus's feet with the costly oil,

Then He turned to the woman and said to Simon, "Do you see this woman? I entered your house; you gave me no water for my feet, but she has washed my feet with her tears and wiped them with the hair of her head. You gave me no kiss, but this woman has not ceased to kiss my feet since the time I came in. You did not anoint my head with oil, but this woman has anointed my feet with fragrant oil. Therefore, I say to you, her sins, which are many, are forgiven, for she loved much. But to whom little is forgiven, the same loves little." (Luke 7:44–47 NKJV)

It was not the many sins that brought her to worship Yeshua, it was her acceptance of the grace she trusted in from the Savior a complete absolution that elicited her pure and unfettered devotion. Her faith was affirmed when; He said to the woman, "Your faith has saved you. Go in peace." Lk 7:50 (NKJV) She demonstrated her faith in His life, she had seen His signs and miracles but better still, she saw His mercy toward all. She knew Him to be beautiful, wonderful, marvelous, and worthy of praise. And He saw the conviction in her worship. "For My yoke is easy and My burden is light." Matt. 11:30 (NKJV) Indeed, she was a freed woman!

Some Christians accept Christ' forgiveness for their petty sins but decline the grace of Yehovah in other sins; those of utter depravity or entrenched character flaws, private sins, we selfishly cling to, while we alternately justify and condemn our indulgence of them. We cling to them as some rightful possession, a badge of martyrdom, a false humility, accepting a personal offense as self-justification. In these we disgrace ourselves and forbid the power of the Master to cleanse us – these are grievous, arrogant acts, full of unbelief and rebellion, an idol unto ourselves, mocking the Master's power. Whatever their portent, the power of the Spirit of Yehovah in the Christian provides freedom from these self-indulgences, to cast down every vain imagination, 2 Cor 10:5 (NKJV) "casting down arguments and every high thing that exalts itself against the knowledge of God;" We have no excuse not to mature and overcome our weaknesses. He is worthy of our sacrificing our character flaws to become even as He is. We will never regret giving up those things which limit our relationship to Christ. As often stated, our primary duty is to love the Lord our God with all our heart, mind, soul, and strength and to love one another (Matt. 22:37). He is not asking us to do something evil or contemptible. Those who defer love recuse themselves into bondage to their greed, unforgiveness, hatred and contemptuous lifestyle. We need to be careful not to miss this dispensation of Yehovah's grace lest we blind our own souls.

> "Therefore I speak to them in parables, because seeing they do not see, and hearing they do not hear, nor do they understand." (Matt. 13:13 NKJV)

This stern warning is equally for us today to ensure our safety and eternal inheritance (Heb. 4:1–2, 2 Cor. 7:1).

Liberty is a two-edged blade, it is not approval to live a venomous, licentious, and immoral life. Many Christians are bitter, judgmental, and not at peace in their relationships with their fellowman. How does the love of Christ Jesus abide in them? We are not to use our freedom in Christ Jesus as a cover for our sin (1 Pet. 2:16), but as willing servants of Yehovah, honoring everyone, loving the brotherhood, fearing Yehovah, and honoring those government authorities appointed by Him. God can turn the hearts of the most callous persons; we, as petitioners of His grace, need only humble ourselves and ask Him to do so.

> Love does no harm to a neighbor; therefore, love is the fulfillment of the law. (Rom. 13:8 NKJV)

When we walk in love, the old debate that it promotes "sloppy agape" is a poor counterargument to the Gospel of Yeshua when one considers how His liberating grace frees His sons and daughters from the tenets of modern-day legalist to become even as He is.

CHAPTER 8

SIN'S AUTHORITY IS BASED IN LAW

In this section, we will address the power of sin and how the Mosaic Law provided the legal authority for sin and death (Rom. 8:2) to operate against us.

> For if those who are of the law are heirs, faith is made void and the promise made of no effect, because the law brings about wrath; for where there is no law there is no transgression. (Rom. 4:14 NKJV)

There are two points I would like to make here:

1. The Law brings wrath. Somehow this statement rings contrary to everything I had assumed about the Law of Yehovah, the Old Testament, even the entirety of the Word of Yehovah. I thought Yehovah wanted to save me, not condemn me. I am glad the Father did not stop at the Law of Moses, or we would be eternal toast.

2. Where there is no Law, there is no transgression. So Law brought transgression because of mankind's weakness; hence, removal of or supersession of the law results in a no-guilt verdict, as there is no law. See Romans 5:13 (NKJV), "For until the law sin was in the world, but sin is not imputed when there is no law." This was a new

revelation to me. Yehovah satisfied the Law and the wrath He had toward us because of our offenses through the life and death of His own Son. He satisfied the penalty for all sin for all time, instituted a New Covenant without the strictures of the Old Covenant, and simultaneously made the Old Covenant laws obsolete so that we could not transgress it. We now can choose to live by faith in His atonement, mercy, and grace through Christ Jesus. He set the law aside, made it inapplicable, so that it was no longer relevant to the New Covenant believer. So once again, where can we find this proof in scripture? Let us start with "Having wiped out the handwriting of requirements that was against us, which was contrary to us. And He has taken it out of the way, having nailed it to the cross" (Col. 2:14 NKJV). Also see Romans 8:2–4.

> For on the one hand there is an annulling of the former commandment because of its weakness and unprofitableness, for the law made nothing perfect; on the other hand, there is the bringing in of a better hope, through which we draw near to God. (Heb. 7:18–19 NJKV)

Also see Hebrews 9:10 and 10:9 and Ephesians 2:15.

There are two spiritual laws contained in Romans 8:2, the Law of the Spirit of Life in Christ Jesus and the Law of Sin and Death. We must recognize that Yehovah nailed the Mosaic Law (Col. 2:14) to the cross of cursing at Calvary. Galatians 3:13 (NKJV) says, "Christ has redeemed us from the curse of the law, having become a curse for us (for it is written, 'Cursed is everyone who hangs on a tree'), that the blessing of Abraham might come upon the Gentiles in Christ Jesus, that we might receive the promise of the Spirit through faith." Yeshua Hamashiach took the holy and lawful wrath of Yehovah destined for sinful man and substituted His life for ours, delivering us from a justifiable damnation that was legally due us. Sins of the flesh have always been sinful and unholy; Jesus did not curse, change, or cancel the Law. He satisfied its penalty that was to be ours, thereby testifying to the condemnation that sin brings. He paid its price. He did not simply wipe it off the slate of judgment, as though it never existed. He satisfied its retribution! Upon His condemnation of fleshly sin and his ensuing suffering as atonement for sin, the Law of Sin and Death was satiated, the souls of men were exhumed from Sheol's grasp by the power of the Blood of Jesus via the Law of the Spirit of Life that we might now live only by the Law of the Spirit. The Law of Moses caused sin to increase that God might extend an overabundance of His grace on us (Rom. 5:20).

> The sting of death is sin, and the strength of sin is the law.
> (1 Cor. 15:56 NKJV)

The first time the Holy Spirit opened my eyes to these scriptures, I was shocked and bewildered. Why would He do that? I thought the Old Testament was meant for our good. "How could the Law be a dreadful thing for us?" Well, as it turns out, it is an incredibly good thing for us because it taught us not to trust in our works but to trust in Christ's work.

> For sin shall not have dominion over you, for you are not
> under law but under grace. (Rom. 6:14 NKJV)

Again, we see that sin's dominion and power over our lives were rooted in the Law. Through the Law of the Spirit of Life in Christ Jesus and the nailing of the laws that were contrary to us to the cross, we now live under grace with power to overcome temptation so that sin has no control over the New Covenant believer. Sin no longer has dominion over those who accept God's grace! We are free from the penalties and the requirements associated with the Law as we keep Yehovah's "first and great commandment" (see Matt. 22:37 NKJV). And should we sin?

> If we confess our sins, He is faithful and just to forgive
> us our sins and to cleanse us from all unrighteousness. (1
> John 1:9 NKJV)

> Therefore, my brethren, you also have become dead to the
> law through the body of Christ, that you may be married

to another—to Him who was raised from the dead, that
we should bear fruit to God. (Rom. 7:4 NKJV)

We who believe in the atoning blood of Christ have become married to
Him, to a New Covenant. Through the Spirit of Life bearing blood that was
given for us, we are now dead to the Law, having died with Christ through
His death and resurrection. Our head is now Christ Jesus, the head of the
church, and we as His body are bound to Him, eternally dwelling in the
Spirit of Life to bear fruit to Yehovah. It is a foolproof way of encapsulating
the believer within a member of the Godhead that keeps us forever from
going astray!

You may ask, as I have, "What if I continue to miss the mark and sin
in heaven as I continue to do in this life?" Remember, the Law is no longer
applicable to you, not now, nor in heaven. Christ Jesus died once for all sin,
for all sins forever. By one offering, He perfected us forever for all time.
Even if we did miss the mark in heaven, His sacrifice delivers perpetually.

But this Man, after He had offered one sacrifice for sins
forever, sat down at the right hand of God, from that time
waiting till His enemies are made His footstool. For by
one offering He has perfected forever those who are being
sanctified. (Heb. 10:12–14 NKJV)

Now, is that great or what? Yehovah delivers us completely and securely.
We have nothing to fear. He is sanctifying us for His own possession. We
serve an awesome God!

But sin, taking opportunity by the commandment,
produced in me all manner of evil desire. For apart from
the law sin was dead. I was alive once without the law, but
when the commandment came, sin revived, and I died.
And the commandment, which was to bring life, I found
to bring death. (Rom. 7:8–10 NKJV)

When Adam was created, all mankind was contained within his seed.
Adam was sinless; hence, we too were sinless before the transgression.

Adam fell at the one commandment issued by God, and death came to all. This reality was amplified by the addition of the Law of Moses; stringent commandments caused sin to increase.

Sin's authority was grounded in the Law, whether that law be the Law given to Moses on Mt. Sinai or the singular restriction given to Adam and Eve in the Garden of Eden, "of the tree of knowledge of good and evil, thou shall not eat." Humanity failed, and sin abounded. It is therefore,

> For by grace you have been saved through faith, and that not of yourselves; it is the gift of God, not of works, lest anyone should boast. (Eph. 2:8 NKJV)

> For He Himself is our peace, who has made both one, and has broken down the middle wall of separation, having abolished in His flesh the enmity, that is, the law of commandments contained in ordinances, so as to create in Himself one new man from the two, thus making peace, and that He might reconcile them both to God in one body through the cross, thereby putting to death the enmity. (Eph. 2:14–15 NKJV)

Sin's authority has now been debased by the work of our Messiah on the cross. He, being perfect and without sin, paid our sin penalty, satiated the wrath of Yehovah that was against us, and abolished the enmity rooted in the commandments of the Law, purchasing our eternal redemption.

The Sovereignty of Yehovah—We Are His Creation

We wonder at what Yehovah is doing. We cannot understand His ways, and therefore we develop strategies, programs, and theologies to corral our beliefs into an acceptable belief system or statement of faith. Thankfully, Yehovah had determined His eternal plan long before we came along, and He continues to reveal its mysteries of our purchase and purpose.

> Shall the clay say to him who forms it, "What are you making?"
>
> Or shall your handiwork say, "He has no hands"? (Isa. 45:9 NKJV)

That is to say, "I am my own maker. I have my own rule and exist by and for myself alone, owing to no one or any other being or God." Man is predisposed to error from his birth, and it does not get much better from there. Fortunately, we have a gracious Father who is intent on disciplining and training up a myriad of misfits and renegade children into sons and daughters for His own possession. It is a daunting endeavor and one that requires our cooperation and submission to the Holy Spirit's leading. We are in training here on earth, and it will continue whenever the Father's kingdom is reestablished on His new heaven and earth, but in the meanwhile, we are being instructed on how to trust the Father. Hebrews 10:14 reveals this instruction program:

> For by one offering He has perfected forever those who are being sanctified. (Heb. 10:14 NKJV)

Our sanctification outlines the Father's purpose for us. We were at once, at one sacrifice, perfected by the blood of Yeshua Hamashiach, but the sanctification part is an ongoing affair, portions of which I personally need significant reminders and retraining.

When I was a young man, establishing a foundation of faith was not straightforward and resolute. While hearing and believing the Gospel, the sirens of the world were persistently calling. Being aware of my failures and doubts presented a continual battle in my mind. I pondered my security in Christ even though my heart was in love with Jesus. Then some years later, the Holy Spirit reminded me of 1 John 3:7 (NKJV) "Little children, let no one deceive you. He who practices righteousness is righteous, just as He is righteous." Whew! What a relief! Even my attempts to be better, though I failed often, were proof that I remained His and that He loved me. That, my friends, is what a loving Savior does. He extends us His grace to live as we,

Work out your own salvation, even with fear and trembling,
for it is God who works in you both to will and to do for
His good pleasure. (Phil. 2:12–13 NKJV)

Even the will to do good is not of ourselves; He gives us that too. We are His possession. He has taken responsibility to secure and deliver us, though we may be allowed to suffer despair, fear, and trembling; eventually, it will undergird our faith in His unseen presence. Hardship encourages us to stay away from sin until we mature, as we learn sins' consequences result in correction or stern discipline. It is an act of Yehovah's mercy toward us to keep us from falling away. King David wrote in the Psalm 23:4c (NKJV), "Your rod and Your staff, they comfort me." This is precisely the Father's intent, to keep us from suffering loss. So much for boasting in our own works.

CHAPTER 9

THE FREEWILL AND THE LAWFUL TITHE

A lot of folks are afraid to discuss the subject of the tithe (a unit of measure meaning a tenth). It's one of those biblical topics that many think defines whether one is truly spiritual or a faithful Christian. Neither is entirely true. The stigma of being a nontither or to object to its onerous imposition in many assemblies is too much for most Christians to dare broach. Some folks proudly announce what faithful tithers they are; others simply nod in affirmation or quietly go along with the prescribed notion of its bound duty. In Matthew 23:23 (NKJV), we come to the only reference by Jesus about the tithe: "Woe to you, scribes and Pharisees, hypocrites! For you pay tithe of mint and anise and cummin, and have neglected the weightier matters of the law: justice and mercy and faith. These you ought to have done, without leaving the others undone." Jesus was speaking only to those who were under the Mosaic Law. As we have stated earlier, only the Hebrews present at Mt. Sinai were given the Law, and then it fell to their descendants to remain under that Law until the time of reformation should come; it was not given to the Gentiles. Here, Yeshua once again states that He was sent only to the House of Israel:

> But He answered and said, "I was not sent except to the lost sheep of the house of Israel." (Matt. 15:24 NKJV)

He lived under the Mosaic Law and would never have told them not to obey the Mosaic Covenant that they were compelled to keep, and He clearly was not speaking to Gentiles who were not party to the Mosaic Covenant.

As we approach this sensitive subject, try to keep in mind that the tithe remains an appropriate measure of giving and that the following is not against the practice of the tithe itself but against the abuses inflicted by the presbytery on the body of Christ who have suffered from its malpractice. We will cover both sides of this touchy topic in sufficient detail, so don't throw the book out until after you have read both sides.

Various Christian denominations and those of various spin-off doctrines (I'll let you figure those out) may no longer preach circumcision or practice animal sacrifices, but a sizable portion of them continue to espouse some of the Mosaic tenets for their financial advantage. These organizations make relentless pleadings and mailings for donations and tithes while claiming evidence of signs, wonders and miracles, angelic manifestations, visions, and spiritual gifts. They make outlandish faith professions and utter vague and questionable prophesies, most without scriptural support or sound doctrine. Though there are legitimate manifestations of all these from time to time, their prominence is generally presented with a good deal of hyperbole. Others send panhandlers on street corners to witness their poverty to the unsaved; I can only imagine what the non-Christians must be thinking when they observe beggars for Jesus acting as though they are being a witness for Christ. I pity the hapless fella sitting at the stoplight who has no clue why he is being solicited to fund some religious organization that can't pay their bills and who has not the slightest inclination to be associated with it. Where is the street preacher who proclaims the kingdom of God without cost? We have displaced faith in the atoning work of the Lord Yeshua Hamashiach with money groveling, theatrics, coercion, and manipulation tactics to keep the program running. We have gone from preaching and worshipping the God who saves us by His grace to promoting personalities, programs, and ecumenical approval through a works-based theology, conveniently contrived through the abuse of Mosaic Covenant tenets solely intended for the nation of Israel's temporary atonement and its Levitical priesthood's sustenance.

How many times have we heard that someone did not have enough faith to believe in God's provision to repay them for their tithe or that His favor or healing is contingent on their obedience to support the ministry? We have heard Malachi 3:10 beat over the heads of the congregants so many times that opposition to its New Covenant and Gentile application is considered near blasphemy. How is it that those who have been freed from the curse of the Law have now been browbeaten to return and try to keep it again? Have these preachers been studying the same Word of God that is presented in the pages of this book? We have missed the Son of Yehovah in our endeavors, as we were blinded by the theology of modern-day religionist who twist scriptures, promising that if you just believe their rhetoric, God will be pleased with you and make you rich, rather than being accepted by Yehovah through the work of our Lord Jesus. Many are promised a tenfold return on the tithe, a guaranteed investment, an appealing morsel to the needy fish whose bait has been craftily situated to obscure the hook (of the Law). Notwithstanding that the Gentile churches were never covenanted or commanded to tithe; that is a different covenant altogether, specifically designed for the tribes of Israel. Gentiles, along with Abram, could and did contribute voluntarily. Sincere Christians have been shamed by accusations they did not have enough faith to receive their requests, presumably because they had sin in their life or lacked the measure of faith that Yehovah has given to all men. They were told they did not trust or love God enough, or if they had paid their tithes, their ship would have come in. Presumably, the blessings of Yehovah were withheld because their 10 percent was not paid or they owed delinquent tithes; healing and miracles could not be received because the tithe was not kept; they broke the law! The shame and dishonor cast upon the laity proved faith in a loving Yehovah incomprehensible to the condemned. How could Yehovah look upon them favorably, forgive them of their failures and sins, or heal them when they felt such condemnation? They were firmly convinced they were not in right standing with Him. This is a works-based heresy that has caused untold damage to believers in Christ Jesus. Rest assured, He is not pleased!

> Therefore, He who supplies the Spirit to you and works miracles among you, does He do it by the works of the law, or by the hearing of faith? (Gal. 3:5 NKJV)

The body of Christ Jesus has been swindled by false prophets because the sheep were not taught the full Gospel of Christ Jesus and because they have not searched out the scriptures themselves to test those things spoken to them (1 Cor. 14:29, 1 John 4:1). Believing the Gospel, that is the Good News part, is the answer to receiving Yehovah's gift of eternal life, favor, and miracles. God will do marvelous things in our lives if we simply trust in His Good News and not the trappings of a hybrid-Mosaic blessings-and-curses doctrine.

A familiar example of the tithe is that of Abram, as described in Genesis 14:18+ and Hebrews 7:1+, where Abram is giving a tithe to one who is a type of the coming Messiah. In Hebrews 7:2–3 (NKJV), Melchizedek is described as "'king of righteousness' and then also king of Salem, meaning 'king of peace,' without father, without mother, without genealogy, having neither beginning of days nor end of life, but made like the Son of God, remains a priest continually." Melchizedek presents us with an earthly, presumably human yet immortal being who foreshadows the Messiah to come. Some believe him to have simply been another mortal man, but that simply does not square with scripture stated in Genesis 14 and Hebrews 7.

> But he whose genealogy is not derived from them received tithes from Abraham and blessed him who had the promises. Now beyond all contradiction the lesser is blessed by the better. Here mortal men receive tithes, but there he receives them, of whom it is witnessed that he lives. (Heb. 7:6–8 NKJV)

Interestingly, Melchizedek received tithes as an immortal being, though presumably human, as he dwelt and served as a priest on this earth. He represents the coming priesthood of Yeshua Hamashiach, and he received a tithe from Abram. We, too, can give tithes to honor Yeshua Hamashiach as a form of our worship, outside of any commandment to do so. It's a freewill offering from a cheerful giver. Not under compulsion but with thanksgiving. And God will bless the giver even as He blessed Abram!

Yeshua Hamashiach's genealogy was partly through Mary, a protracted descendant of King David via Nathan, and partly through the Holy Spirit (Yehovah incarnate), who now holds the promises for us as being the Seed of Abraham (Gal. 3:16). He is the referenced endless life (Heb. 7:16),who came not according to the law of a fleshly commandment:

> For it is evident that our Lord arose from Judah, of which tribe Moses spoke nothing concerning priesthood. And it is yet far more evident if, in the likeness of Melchizedek, there arises another priest who has come, not according to the law of a fleshly commandment, but according to the power of an endless life. For He testifies: "You are a priest forever according to the order of Melchizedek." (Heb. 7:14–17 NKJV)

Here, we are introduced again to the concept that our deliverance and deliverer are not provisioned via a lawful commandment but by His divine will and love for His creation and that it was done according to the power of an endless life. As there is only one endless life, we see that Yehovah's redemption of mankind extends from himself alone, God made flesh—Immanuel. So why this reference of God's divine will to choose our redemption? It's the same free will that we all can employ to offer thanksgiving, praise, and funding to promote His gospel of grace. We are to be life partners in working our Father's fields, fields that are ready for harvest.

It would be another 430 years before the tithe moved from the freewill offering that Abram gave to Melchizedek to become a part of the Mosaic Law and a source of funding for the nation's theocratic governance. The tithe would no longer be considered a freewill offering to the Hebrew children; however, it was not required those forty years while wandering in the desert but only after the children of Israel had been given and possessed the lands, crops sown and reaped. At which time the onus was on the heart of the tither to ensure they were giving with a heart of thanksgiving and worship and not with one of resentment. Today, though we may not be under a tithe commandment to honor the work of the Lord, we can choose without compulsion how we want to give to the work of the gospel and ensure our attitude of worship is not impinged in honoring our Savior.

Abram honored the priest Melchizedek with a tithe prior to the Law of Moses as a freewill offering because Melchizedek first blessed Abram, and

Abram knew Yehovah was with Melchizedek simply by the blessing that Melchizedek bestowed. Given the state of Melchizedek, apparently being of immortal origin, his notoriety and righteous priesthood would have been known in the region, and as the terebinth trees of Mamre (Hebron), where Abram dwelt, lay approximately twenty-one miles south of Jerusalem, it is possible that Abram may have known Melchizedek beforehand. When upon Abram's return from rescuing Lot, he is approached by Melchizedek in Genesis 14:18–20,

> Then Melchizedek king of Salem brought out bread and wine; he was the priest of God Most High. And he blessed him and said: "Blessed be Abram of God Most High, Possessor of heaven and earth; And blessed be God Most High, who has delivered your enemies into your hand." And he gave him a tithe of all. (Gen. 14:18–20 NKJV)

First we see that Yehovah blesses Abram, and by extension, God blesses His children! Abram recognized Melchizedek's position of being the Most High's priest when he brought out the bread (body) and wine (blood), which symbolized the redemptive sacrifice of the coming Messiah. They both understood the sacrificial atonement through the promised Messiah! Abram honored Melchizedek's person, king of righteousness, king of peace. Abram esteemed the representative of the most-high God because he saw Melchizedek's faith in Yehovah's redemptive plan as represented in the implements. Though Abram's gift was not an obligation by commandment, and as it was freely bestowed, what a missed opportunity if Abram had chosen not to give a tenth to Melchizedek! Abram's faith was stirred by Melchizedek's blessing! By faith, Abram accepted the blessing as from Yehovah, and he bestowed a gift of honor and of worship unto Yehovah for the blessing he had received. Abram believed every word that Melchizedek spoke to him, just as Abram had previously believed God, and it was counted to him as righteousness.

Abram could have given more or less than the tithe. As it was, it would later become the divine portion used in the Mosaic Covenant some 430 years later. Israel was to become a theocratic form of government; tithes and freewill offerings were the sole means of funding for that government whose head was Yehovah. Citizens and subjects pay homage and duty to those who govern over them as a means of submission, blessing, protection, and honor. Some pay to those who rule over them in government, or who minister to them, reluctantly, deceptively, or with contempt. Our rendering attitude to those in need and those in ministry speaks clearly of the state of our relationship with the Father. If we love the Father, we will be in fellowship with Him to support those who work on His behalf and give in accordance with our ability. At times, our passion to give may surpass our current ability to give. Harvests are cyclical; so too are our seasons and abilities. God looks upon the heart and does not condemn those who are so constrained. For those who struggled financially, there was a prescribed limit for the poor even within the lawful tithe, sufficient to meet the needs of the temple and its attendants and sufficient to the ability of the nation to provide them adequate support, no matter their station in life. Yehovah was their supplier, just as he is ours; relative to each member, He provides ability and blessing. The tithe was Yehovah's measure for their governance and feasts, yet those who were poor were permitted exemptions to some of the Law's applications (Lev. 5:7, 11;12:8). The Old Covenant was interlaced with reverence for Yehovah and suitable to the attendee, that they might fear Him and keep His commands. It was also full of God's mercy and provision for the nation and its less fortunate, that He might bless them.

> And the Levite, because he has no portion nor inheritance with you, and the stranger and the fatherless and the widow who are within your gates, may come and eat and be satisfied, that the Lord your God may bless you in all the work of your hand which you do. (Deut. 14:29 NKJV)

Our Father cares for those who minister to Him and for the destitute, fatherless, and widows. As followers of Yeshua, we can do no less.

In Mark 12:41–40, Jesus recognizes the poor widow who gave two mites, just a few cents in today's market. It was all she had to live on, 100 percent of her life's savings, yet she gave it with a heart full of thanksgiving and faith in Yehovah's provision. Whether she lived or died, her trust rested completely in Him. She wasn't singing or dancing in her impoverished state.

It was her position in life, yet her heart remained resolute in worship and thanksgiving. Yeshua noticed her. He knew her poverty. Better still, He knew her gracious attitude of worship.

There was no command to tithe up until Moses. However, up until that time, there would have been tithes given, as Abram clearly made a tithe to Melchizedek. He either learned it from his forefathers, or perhaps he instituted it; we simply don't know. The few instances recorded were either by Abram or Jacob (Gen. 28:22), though there is no evidence Abram ever tithed again or that Jacob fulfilled his vow, nor to whom he would have paid it. Though here again, if Melchizedek were around, he would undoubtedly have been an excellent choice. Nonetheless, from the time of Adam to Moses, a period of about 2,500 years, there were only freewill offerings. So what changed? The Mosaic Law was added, and the Book of the Law changed the tithe from a freewill gift to that of a commandment for the Hebrew children. Thereafter, the Mosaic Law was only in force for about 1,500 years, from the moment Moses received the Law at Mt. Sinai up until the crucifixion of Yeshua Hamashiach, at which time the Law was fulfilled. Jesus then set it aside (Heb. 10:9). This fact is nonnegotiable. The Old Covenant cannot coexist in authority with the New Covenant. The hearer and the reader must choose which covenant they will follow. The Messianic Hebrew was at that time liberated from the Law of Moses, and those who continue in serving the tabernacle, or the Mosaic system, will continue to be judged according to the Law. On the other hand, the teachings of righteousness, love, and worship, which were contained within the Law of Moses that the prophets taught, were originally derived from and continue within the preeminent commandment of Matthew 22:37+, not vice versa.

Even as Melchizedek received Abram's freewill tithe, tithes can be offered today on behalf of Christ Jesus to promote the work of the gospel. We can support ministries, the needy, widows, orphans, and many other suitable causes, but they should not be offered with respect to the Law of Moses. One is an offering of thanksgiving, honor, and reverence with no compulsion, while the other is a function of compliance to the commandment according to the Law of Mt. Sinai (a.k.a. the Old Covenant). There are serious consequences for not keeping all the Law.

For whoever shall keep the whole law, and yet stumble in one point, he is guilty of all. (James 2:10 NKJV)

And for offending the Spirit of Grace,

Anyone who has rejected Moses' law dies without mercy on the testimony of two or three witnesses. Of how much worse punishment, do you suppose, will he be thought worthy who has trampled the Son of God underfoot, counted the blood of the covenant by which he was sanctified a common thing, and insulted the Spirit of grace? (Heb. 10:28–29 NKJV)

Oddly enough, it is the same religious systems present today, cut from the same Pharisaic cloth, that glorify the tithe giver as a super Christian.

"Take heed that you do not do your charitable deeds before men, to be seen by them. Otherwise, you have no reward from your Father in heaven. Therefore, when you do a charitable deed, do not sound a trumpet before you as the hypocrites do in the synagogues and in the streets, that they may have glory from men." (Matt. 6:1–2 NKJV).

I have seen the parading of gifts before the congregation with much ballyhoo, musical marches, and drama-infused fundraisers over the years, even with trumpets. Some ministries have extracted Old Covenant tithing laws that were never incumbent upon the Gentile believer and use it to manipulate their congregation. This abuse is rampant in many Christian assemblies and cults today. Regardless, Yehovah loves a cheerful giver, and we have plenty of reason to give cheerfully as we recognize that we have been forgiven much; therefore, we also should love much. When we worship Yehovah with our hearts, our giving will follow freely to bless those who minister and those in need. And

He who sees in secret will reward you openly (Matt. 6:4b NKJV).

New Covenant giving is well defined in the following:
> But this I say: He who sows sparingly will also reap sparingly, and he who sows bountifully will also reap bountifully. So let each one give as he purposes in his heart, not grudgingly or of necessity; for God loves a cheerful giver. (2 Cor. 9:6–7 NKJV)

There is no shortage of Yehovah's power to supply abundance to the cheerful giver. Yehovah wants to bless us, and He wants us to bless others—in every good work.

Let's look at how the apostle Paul conducted himself as a Messianic Hebrew and what he instructed others about giving. The apostle Paul was a Benjamite, not a Levite, and therefore was not entitled to receive tithes, as only Levites were authorized to receive tithes. Paul had a right to make a living from the gospel (1 Cor. 9:14–15), though he deferred it, preferring not to be a burden. He worked with his own hands and supported some of those who traveled with him. Paul gave freely to any who had need. And on occasion, he instructed that a collection for the saints be gathered from those in Galatia and Corinth (1 Cor. 16:1–3), from those who had the ability to give, and that it be taken to those in Jerusalem. He was not gathering funds to donate to the desecrated temple rebuilding fund. It was for the Hebrew Christians who were being hunted down, thrown into prisons, beaten and/or put to death by the religious authorities who served the local church, er, the temple. When tribulation arose against the Messianic Hebrews throughout Israel, temple and synagogue attendances dropped (John 12:11), along with their revenue stream. When the de facto government of Israel rejected their Messiah, temple gatherings and the tithes financing the Levitical system of governance were also severely affected. It would be unreasonable to think the first-century believers were attending Sabbath services at the temple or local synagogue, as they lived in constant fear of persecution and death. Nor would they support a religious system that had been visibly desecrated and set aside. Instead, the first-century believers met from house to house because it was the prudent thing to do. Upon the death of God's Son, the holy of holies veil was destroyed by Yehovah's earthquake, signaling the end of the Old Covenant sacrificial system. The rest of the temple was destroyed in AD 70. Yeshua Hamashiach was the long-awaited Lamb of God. The final Day of Atonement (Yom Kippur, Lev. 16) had been completed, and the atoning sacrifices for the sins of the Jewish nation (Heb. 10:18) ceased. The Lamb of Yehovah had been sacrificed! Everything changed!

On a sidenote, Jesus was born into the tribe of Judah. He, too, was not a Levite and therefore never received a tithe under the Mosaic Law. Jesus did receive gifts and alms during His ministry, as overseen by Judas Iscariot. Melchizedek, a foreshadowing of Yeshua Hamashiach, received a tithe though he was not under the Law. It appears we are free to honor the Lord just as Abram was, not by commandment but by choice. Today, we may not be funding the operation of a theocratic government, Levitical priesthood, or Melchizedek; we remain at liberty to give according to our ability and preference.

Though the Law and the tithe have been set aside for the Messianic Hebrew (a.k.a. Christian), its doctrine continues to be hawked and abused in many churches as being incumbent upon the Christian. Today, we have the liberty to give sparingly or lavishly, only that it should be a gift of thanksgiving and worship. We may use the measure of the tithe, but there is no requirement or commandment for the New Covenant believer to abide by the Mosaic Law. All tithes and alms giving should be given in honor, much like Abram did toward Melchizedek—the type of Christ to come. We can support those who faithfully minister the gospel or give to those in the body who lack necessities, to the poor and needy, widows, orphans, and so on, whether within or outside of the assembly. Jesus gave to all men liberally. Even to the Samaritan woman He gave eternal life (John 4). Then He gave His life for all. Let us not strain at the gnat of the size of the gift when the Lord has called us to peace.

On a lighter note, today, most of us pay a sizable portion larger than the tithe to our governments for city, state, county, and federal governance. Yehovah knows how to run an efficient government on 10 percent. Our governments seem to do far less with higher percentages. Some may think the tithe as an onerous burden, but in view of its purpose toward sin atonement and governance of the nation of Israel, it was significantly less a burden than our modern governments tax policies. The tithe has simply been misplaced, misrepresented, and foisted upon the body of Christ, often unscrupulously. Of course, Israel's sweet deal ended when the children of Israel declared that they wanted a king like all the other pagan nations, which angered the Lord, so He relented to their complaining and gave them one—King Saul, who subjugated them, taxed them, seized their lands, and conscripted their sons for government use (1 Sam. 8:11–18). And the world's governments have continued the practice ever since.

Telemarketing Preachers

It has been my unfortunate experience to have heard faith, prosperity, and prophetic preachers make pretentious and ridiculous proclamations, the blind leading the blind, with followers abandoning sound doctrine for deceitful, ear-tickling promises. Greed became a prominent feature of the evangelical faith movement, often disguised as a spiritual right of the believer to reach out and take hold of the promises of God's abundance and prosperity. As a result, many Christians were dismayed when their proclamation of faith did not happen. Millions of people sowed billions of dollars to televangelists and churches under the pretense of supporting a ministry that promoted the idea that financial obedience would produce a sizable financial harvest. They were instructed to be the head and not the tail, to overcome poverty and assume their rightful position in Christ as possessors of the land. "All to the glory of God!" they exclaimed. Or was it? As it was, the mercy of Yehovah kept many from spiritual ruin by not allowing their proclamations to come to fruition and exposing the fruitlessness and deceit of prosperity teachers. True wealth and prosperity are only obtained in an intimate relationship with Yehovah by the Holy Spirit; everything else is injurious deception. It seemed much of Christendom ran rampant, naming and claiming houses, boats, planes, and riches instead of living, loving, rejoicing in, and believing in the Son Yehovah has sent, wherein true prosperity exists. Preachers got rich, false prophets got notoriety, the flock got fleeced, and once again Yeshua Hamashiach got missed.

When spiritual growth has been shunted by poor theology, the onerous building program often serves well as a congregational unifier; if they can't grow spiritually, then maybe a building program will create the appearance of it. Hence, the building committee and their hired circuit solicitor salesman are called in to promote the mission, enlarge the tent of meeting, build schools, and encourage congregants to make vows before Yehovah to pay for bigger edifices and to finance programs. This leads to more multimedia sales presentations and their associated debt, which the congregants become obliged to absorb, all under the guise of "not forsaking the assembling of ourselves together, as is the manner of some" (Heb. 10:25 NKJV). The apostolic writers neglected to mention the unwritten commandment, "Go ye into all the world and build idolatrous places to worship." We now have entertainment facilities we like to call churches, a locale to corral the masses for ear tickling and fleecing, a mockery of a true Sabbath's rest. Observing the Lord's Day has become more taxing than the regular workday, and it is of little wonder people avoid the religious affair altogether. These religious indoctrination centers, known as corporations, have duped well-intentioned Christians to bow at the feet of the ecumenical squad, pastoral bias, and denominational creed to pay indulgences (tithes) and bequeath inheritances, insurance policies, and livelihood to religious organizations who have usurped the Law of Yehovah through deceit and coercion. Strangely enough, all the apostles and Yeshua must have missed that doctrinal instruction. Yehovah authorized only one temple for the Hebrew people. Accordingly, the only temple authorized by God today resides within the believing heart.

> "Woe to you, blind guides, who say, whoever swears by the temple, it is nothing; but whoever swears by the gold of the temple, he is obliged to perform it.' Fools and blind! For which is greater, the gold or the temple that sanctifies the gold?" (Matt. 23:16–17 NKJV)

This is a serious indictment against those who serve the altar, or the church, for lucre. The Word of Yehovah reminds us that we are His temple (1 Cor. 3:16–17, Eph. 2:21, Rom. 8:9) and that we are to bring forth "'genuineness of your faith, being much more precious than gold that perishes, though it is tested by fire, may be found to praise, honor, and glory at the revelation of Jesus Christ" (1 Pet. 1:7 NKJV). It is the heart altar of the giver that sanctifies the offering!

It is an unfortunate truth about modern-day theology that the ecumenical mindset of many is one of governance and greed, to shepherd complacent sheep and not the maturing of soldiers for Christ with sound biblical doctrine. Without a motivation to fall further in love with their Savior, weighted down by legalism, doctrines of men and bylaws, the body of Christ is suffering at the very hands designed to instruct it in righteousness and inspire pursuit of the Spirit of Life in Christ Jesus.

Where Is the Storehouse?

For those churches that religiously collect the tithe, they seldom exercise any of the responsibilities associated with its distribution, nor the support of the entire ministerial team, as did the Levitical priesthood. Notwithstanding the fact that there can be no Gentile Levites, it is, however, a curious observation. They do not distribute the tithe as contained in the laws of Leviticus; there is no storehouse of agricultural goods or distribution to all members of the ministry. The elderly, widows, and orphans are neglected, and most of the church volunteers are unpaid. The choir, deacons, and Sunday school teachers are unpaid. Everyone from the day care attendant to the usher, elder, secretary, and maintenance worker is typically considered a volunteer. That was not the case with the Hebrew nation, wherein the entire tribe of Levi, one tribe out of twelve, had their portion in the tithes, offerings, and sacrifices (Deut. 18:1+). The tithe, alms, and sacrifices were the Levites' only means of support for being Yehovah's ministers in His theocracy.

Cornelius presents us with some insight into the character of man that Yehovah honors, "a devout man and one who feared God with all his household, who gave alms generously to the people, and prayed to God always" (Acts 10:2 NKJV).

Roman centurions were not typically known as the best of associates; however, we have an exception in Cornelius, who feared the God of the Hebrews along with his whole household. Cornelius had a firm conviction about a loving and just God, and his convictions extended to the members of his household. Cornelius trusted in God with absolute confidence. His prayer life and generosity rose as a memorial before Yehovah because of his respect for and attitude of worship to the unseen God of the Hebrews. Cornelius was not bound by the law of the tithe; he gave freely and lavishly. He supported those in need without a command to do so. He was not coerced by fear or manipulation or intimidated by a curse; Cornelius simply loved, believed in, and revered the one true Yehovah. His actions flowed willingly from his heart.

> So let each one give as he purposes in his heart, not grudgingly or of necessity; for God loves a cheerful giver. (2 Cor. 9:7 NKJV)

> "Do not lay up for yourselves treasures on earth, where moth and rust destroy and where thieves break in and steal; but lay up for yourselves treasures in heaven, where neither moth nor rust destroys and where thieves do not break in and steal. For where your treasure is, there your heart will be also." (Matt 6:19–21 NKJV)

In contrast to the obligatory tithe, after his conversion, the apostle Paul encouraged the gathering of alms for the saints who were suffering persecution in Jerusalem (2 Cor. 9:1+). Paul did not press them for a tithe, nor did any of the apostles ever request such thereafter. The alms he received were not donated to the Jewish Temple, as the earthly holy of holies' massive curtain had been torn by Yehovah (Matt. 27:51) and the walls made irreparable. To the contrary, Paul ministered to the very persons the religious leaders were persecuting for accepting Jesus as their Messiah and the gospel of liberty from bondage to the Law.

Paul, being a prior associate of the Sanhedrin, knew the holy of holies had been destroyed and that there was no longer a venue for an earthly high priest after the order of Aaron to offer the annual Passover sacrifice for the nation. Yehovah closed that door forever on the day of Jesus Christ's death with an earthquake that tore the veil in two from before the presence of Yehovah. That veil was symbolic of the veil that covered Moses's face when he received the Law on Mt. Sinai, whose glory—that is, the Law's glory—was vanishing away (Hebrews 8:13). Now it has diminished in glory and in practice. When God tore that veil, it became impossible for the Mosaic Law to continue; its purpose had been fulfilled. There would be no purpose in donating monies to the operation of the remaining Levitical order that denied the Messiah. One can only imagine the impact of multitudes leaving the Mosaic system on the temple. The New Covenant had been consummated, and there was no need for the Messianic Hebrews to continue to support a priesthood that had been closed by Yehovah, or else Paul would have required a tithe instead of the gathering of alms, and he would have given it to the priesthood, but he did not. He gave the love gift to the saints in Jerusalem (1 Cor. 16:1–3). Yeshua Hamashiach's death denoted the end of the Law by the establishment of the New Covenant (Hebrews 8:13, 10:9).

CHAPTER 10

SUFFICIENCY THROUGH GRACE

A works-based justification rejects our Father's mercy and grace in our lives; it is a hubris that offends the Spirit of Grace and denies Yehovah's redemptive power. Furthermore, it constrains the power of Yehovah from manifesting His glory in answered prayers, signs, wonders, healings, and salvations, to effectively minister His will to our benefit. It quenches faith in Yehovah's mercy and goodness. Yehovah made a way to pour out His riches upon us absent a works-based justification (Eph. 2:8). The Law exposed man's insufficiency to keep Yehovah's commands and left us with a sense of inadequacy and despair. That which constrains us inhibits us from trusting, honoring and glorifying the Father. Unless our choice to love Him is unfettered, unencumbered by debt of sin, shame, or coercion, it cannot produce perfect love and devotion. If we fear condemnation or judgment, we are not yet perfected in love (1 John 4:18).

> Love has been perfected among us in this: that we may have boldness in the day of judgment; because as He is, so are we in this world. There is no fear in love; but perfect love casts out fear, because fear involves torment. But he who fears has not been made perfect in love. We love Him because He first loved us. (1 John 4:17–20 NKJV)

When I know that there is no mandate to coerce devotion, then I am free to choose life or death again, to love or despise again, to obey or disobey again. Yehovah desires communion with us, to know His goodness; resulting in our praise and worship of Him in spirit and truth. His goodness and mercy are free to those who seek to know and love Him. Correct knowledge of the Lord will produce hearts of thanksgiving and worship.

> Jesus said to him, "Have I been with you so long, and yet you have not known Me, Philip? He who has seen Me has seen the Father; so how can you say, 'Show us the Father'?" (John 14:9 NKJV)

Surely, we have seen the Father's goodness innumerable times. Surely, we know His character. Why restrain Him from pouring out His grace upon us by reverting to the Law?

> My people are destroyed for lack of knowledge. Because you have rejected knowledge. (Hosea 4:6 NKJV)

Here again, we see that it is incumbent upon us to choose what we will believe about Jesus and the Father. We serve an awesome God who loves us infinitely. We are justified by His grace through faith in Messiah (Eph. 2:8).

It is human to try to justify ourselves before others, and sometimes we may even try to lie to ourselves about our own merit. We strive to be good; we want to do well, to say the right things to convince ourselves and others of our own self-worth. Alternately, we attempt to assuage our guilt by imposing some element of self-discipline, setting goals, curbing habits, and so forth to establish some self-worth and validation. However, no amount of self-correction, sacrifice, or work can ever justify us before God. Our sufficiency does not lie within ourselves or our works; our sufficiency comes only from being filled with God's Holy Spirit.

> And we have such trust through Christ toward God. Not that we are sufficient of ourselves to think of anything as being from ourselves, but our sufficiency is from God, who also made us sufficient as ministers of the New Covenant, not of the letter but of the Spirit; for the letter kills, but the Spirit gives life. (2 Cor. 3:4–6 NKJV)

We have seen this comparison before over in Romans 8:2, as the Spirit of Life and the Law of Sin and Death.

When Yehovah said, "Let there be light" (Gen. 1:3 NKJV), it was not a request from another entity; it was a proclamation to bring forth light of His own person, an infinite creative power, a state of being to come forth from nothing into a place of existence. Our sufficiency and newness of life is guaranteed by the Law of the Spirit of Life, just as Lazarus came forth from the tomb; so shall we come forth to love the Lord our God with all our hearts, soul, mind, and body. He will affect our hearts with His glorious Holy Spirit through Christ Jesus, that we will have no reluctance to give over our lives, love, and worship. "Have I been with you so long, and yet you have not known Me" (John 14:9 NKJV). He is far more worthy than we can ever comprehend. We will never find the sum of His beauty, power, and dominion. We can rest in His faithfulness and goodness to keep us secure for His own delight (Ps. 121:7–8).

The apostle Peter tried to do the right things, but he did not always succeed. Our attempts to self-justify become laws unto ourselves, often causing more frustration than good. Our misguided attempts to keep portions of the Mosaic Law, mingled in with the message of grace, will only serve to diminish the power of the grace of Yehovah. We make lighthearted commentary of Peter's humanity because we think we would never act in such a manner; we unwittingly pass judgment on Peter. But if we look closer, we may see that we can all identify with his angst and frustration. Peter, often portrayed as a crusty fisherman, desperately wanted to be of worth to Messiah; he wanted to be somebody for Jesus. However, his humanity kept getting in the way. How was he to be adequate to the task? We will take a longer look at Peter, his bravado, his temper, his envy, but what makes him of significance was his transformation through the Holy Spirit to an apostle who gave over his life, day by day, for the gospel and who wrote two books full of wisdom and grace. Peter's Hebrew roots and culture had been severely altered by the Godman, through his early discipleship trials to his vision at Joppa and at Cornelius house to the Gentiles receiving the baptism in the Holy Spirit; everything was changed by the consummated New Covenant. It is not as though doing the will of the Father is that difficult, but like Peter, we simply must agree to let Him lead us and trust in His Word to empower His resurrection power to change and keep us. If Peter can be transformed from the rascal that he once was to the apostle of Christ that Yehovah made of him, He will transform us today as well. When we cooperate with the working of the Holy Spirit to work out our deficiencies and allow Christ Jesus to be our sufficiency, we please the Father.

> Therefore, my brethren, you also have become dead to the law through the body of Christ. (Rom. 7:4 NKJV)

I repeat: we are dead to the Law through Yeshua's death because we need to be dead to the Law. We simply cannot live up to its requirements. Yeshua performed the Law's requirements perfectly, and by being sacrificed as holy, His death passed judgment on fleshly sin. He condemned it (Rom. 8:3) by being righteous. If Yeshua had not been righteous, sin would not have been judged, but by declaring sin as sinful, He declared the Law as perfect and good and then set it aside, terminating the Law's right to condemn us because He had been condemned in our place, that the Spirit of Life in Christ Jesus might live in us. Righteous conduct convicts and condemns unrighteous conduct. It is the declaration of righteousness from God that convicts.

> For when we were in the flesh, the sinful passions which were aroused by the law were at work in our members to bear fruit to death. But now we have been delivered from the law, having died to what we were once held, so that we should serve in the newness of the Spirit and not in the oldness of the letter. (Rom. 7:5–6 NKJV)

Our sufficiency is now in newness of the Spirit, being dead to the law because, as Jesus died on our behalf, so we died with Him. Again, did you catch the statement that we have been delivered from the Law and that death is the fruit of not keeping the Law?

Romans 8:15 (NKJV) says "For you did not receive the spirit of bondage again to fear, but you received the Spirit of adoption by whom we cry out, 'Abba, Father.'" Now that is just awesome deliverance. Liberation from the Mosaic Covenant, the Law of Sin and Death and adoption whereby we cry, "Daddy!" We, like Jesus, can cherish the Father as our own. He greatly desires a Father/child relationship with us. Can you dare to imagine such a relationship? Has your life been scarred by poor examples or failed relationships? Allow the Spirit of Life to set you free from fear and learn to love wholeheartedly. We are no longer subject to the Law's wrath.

> For God did not appoint us to wrath, but to obtain salvation through our Lord Jesus Christ, who died for us, that whether we wake or sleep, we should live together with Him. (1 Thess. 5:9 NKJV)

We are free to love Him today and forevermore! It was not just the cessation of the Law from which we were liberated but also the gripping fear of failure and judgment that we are no longer subject.

> There is no fear in love; but perfect love casts out fear, because fear involves torment. But he who fears has not been made perfect in love. (1 John 4:18 NKJV)

We fear because we are still walking after the flesh nature. If we continue to seek fleshly pleasures, impure thoughts, and conversation, we are sinning willfully, and the Holy Spirit will continue to convict us of that sin, and we will feel separation from the Father. We simply need to repent and walk in His forgiveness. We always have an advocate with the Father through Christ Jesus (1 John 1:9, 2:1), but we must learn to choose to reject temptation and grow in His grace and strength. It is very much a growing process, a sanctification process. Once we have repented of a particular sin, we will not feel conviction regarding that error from the Holy Spirit again. However, the enemy will continue to condemn us until we have grown strong in our trust in the Lord's grace to recognize and rebuke the liar. If, however, we have no knowledge of sin, we must examine closely where the condemnation is rooted. Sometimes our condemnation is rooted in our culture, other persons, or doctrinal error that cannot be substantiated in the New Covenant. A little time in prayer, scripture study, and reflection creates an opportunity for the Holy Spirit to give us wisdom and freedom in the matter. If we hold on to Old Covenant Law that has been superseded, it will only condemn us. Faith and knowledge of the New Covenant scriptures are required to accept our liberation and stand firm against the onslaught of guilt, to cast down vain imaginations, and to remain steadfast in our Lord's sufficiency on your behalf (2 Cor. 5:17–18). We are engaged in a battle for the mind and soul against dark forces.

> For the weapons of our warfare are not carnal but mighty in God for pulling down strongholds, casting down arguments and every high thing that exalts itself against the knowledge of God, bringing every thought into captivity to the obedience of Christ, and being ready to punish all disobedience when your obedience is fulfilled. (2 Cor. 10:4–6 NKJV)

The children of Israel were confronted with theological conflict and debate regarding Messiah, though they experienced His innumerable miracles and teachings and saw how He met every prophecy of the coming Messiah. Many did not esteem His authority as greater than the Mosaic Law, thereby voiding their faith in Him and their redemption (Gal. 5:4). If we do not know the full truth of the New Covenant, we will continue to fall prey to the condemnation of the Law and suffer similar loss. Our adversaries, even those in religious circles, will wage war against our minds, causing us to question the precepts of our liberty in Christ and keep us from standing on the truth, just as the Pharisees and Sadducees did against the Messianic Jews. Weakness of faith in the promises of Yehovah will cause us to waver by doubting the very promises Yehovah made to Abraham and to his Seed. Sinful flesh brings condemnation and guilt, but the Comforter, the Holy Spirit, brings conviction, correction, and peace. Repentance is the key that enables us to continue walking with Yeshua Hamashiach in love and with power to overcome our enemies' accusations and temptation (Luke 10:19). When we love Him more than ourselves and our fleshly desires, we will trust in and keep His commandments (Matt. 22:37), and we will move from fear to faith, knowing that His blood continually cleanses us from all unrighteousness (1 John 1:9). As His sons and daughters, He gently leads and corrects us by His Spirit (Rom. 8:14–16).

Now that we know our justification and our sufficiency are in Yeshua Hamashiach, is there a commandment that we should honor, Yehovah?

> Jesus said to him, "You shall love the Lord your God with
> all your heart, with all your soul, and with all your mind."
> This is the first and great commandment. And the second
> is like it: You shall love your neighbor as yourself." On these
> two commandments hang all the Law and the Prophets.
> (Matt. 22:37–40 NKJV)

Notice that neither of these two commands are quoted directly from the original Decalogue (Ten Commandments). Nonetheless, they preceded the Law of Moses and were evidenced by God's creation of all things. His glory and beauty are spread across eternity, manifesting His presence and His kingdom's eternal traits, testifying of His goodness and loving kindness. Selflessly loving and serving the Father was the theme of His kingdom long before He created the physical heavens and earth. Yehovah has always been perfect, holy, and exceedingly beautiful in all respects. His divine attributes and law of love preceded the Mosaic Law and is the fountain from which our redemption flows. Love does not hang on the Law and the prophets; it does not receive its power from lawful commands that we are incapable of keeping. It is a willful trust and faith that compels our obedience to Yehovah's commands. To love Him and our fellow man underpins our obedience to the Father. Love is the chalice of devotion we pour out to honor Him. Love is the nature of the Father, for all mercy, kindness, and love originate in Him. To refuse our Father's commandment is to reject His fellowship, as displayed in the Gospel of John.

> If we say that we have fellowship with Him, and walk in
> darkness, we lie and do not practice the truth. (1 John 1:6
> NKJV)

> He who does not love does not know God, for God is love.
> (1 John 4:8 NKJV)

Man's proclivity to error and weakness resulted in our inability to keep the Law and produced in us fear, torment, spiritual darkness, and hardness of heart, blinding us to the true character of Yehovah. The Law and prophets, as tutors, directed us back to a proper understanding and maturity in Yehovah's grace, foretelling a better covenant than the Mosaic Law, away from one that was fading away to a New Covenant full of grace and mercy.

> Stand fast therefore in the liberty wherewith Christ has made us free and be not entangled again with the yoke of bondages. ... Christ is become of no effect unto you, whosoever of you are justified by the law; ye are fallen from grace. for we through the Spirit wait for the hope of righteousness by faith. (Gal. 5:1, 4, 5 NKJV)

Oh what a glorious Redeemer we have! I pray that you will lay hold of and embrace the liberty our Lord Jesus obtained for you. By His grace and mercy alone, we are made children of Yehovah.

> For by grace you have been saved through faith, and that not of yourselves; it is the gift of God, not of works, lest anyone should boast. (Eph. 2:8 NKJV)

CHAPTER 11

THE PROGRESSION OF LOVE

Life is wonderful, yet life is not always convenient, and those who are not grounded in an intimate relationship with the Father, based on trust and faith, will eventually lose confidence in His affection and risk going astray like sheep. The apostle Peter certainly experienced his share of tribulations, though his mannerisms undoubtedly contributed to his being used as an example for our learning. Just as we experience moments of desperation, sickness, sorrow for departed loved ones, days of conflict, and persecution, they too have a way of revealing one's character and convictions. After Peter denied Christ Jesus three times during his trial, Peter fled for his life, fearful and bewildered. Later, the ensuing waves of guilt, doubt, and accusations pummeled Peter's mind. Those who have served Christ for any length of time know that our enemy relentlessly assails us, just as Peter's was, bidding us to deny our faith, our hope and trust in Messiah, and to abandon our tattered relationship with the Father.

> "He who has seen Me has seen the Father; so how can you
> say, 'Show us the Father'?" (John 14:9)

Consider for a moment what we know of Jesus: He was kind, merciful, miraculous, tender, confrontational, forgiving, and relatable. Hebrews 4:15 (NKJV) expresses His humanity. Oddly, Yehovah incarnate is quite a bit like us; "For we do not have a High Priest who cannot sympathize with our weaknesses, but was in all points tempted as we are, yet without sin."

Yehovah did not send His Son to earth so that He could understand what it feels like to be human. He designed and created man. He knows us intimately. He came that we might know Him personally, face-to-face. Jesus came to earth that we might understand that Yehovah has feelings and desires like we do. We forget that when He formed man in His image, He formed us after Himself.

> Then God said, "Let Us make man in Our image, according to Our likeness; let them have dominion over the fish of the sea, over the birds of the air, and over the cattle, over all the earth and over every creeping thing that creeps on the earth." (Gen. 1:26 NKJV)

Jesus knew our distresses, our fears, and all things common to humanity. He suffered as we suffer but did not lose sight of his relation to the Father; Jesus told us that He and the Father are One. "I am in the Father and the Father in Me" (John 14:10). Knowing Jesus's earthly trials, his humanity and divinity, enables us to trust in and approach the Father. He created us in His image, so relating to us is as easy as talking to Himself. He knows you, inside and out, top to bottom, good, bad, the whole of you. Idols of wood and stone cannot know you, nor can other humans know the deepest parts of you, but the Father understands every intimate detail. He knit you together in your mother's womb before you ever knew His existence. Intimacy with you is Yehovah's desire and pleasure. Watching after and caring for you is His personal responsibility; He makes us His business. He keeps His promises. He holds us in the palm of His hands. Winds may assail us, storms will rage, and death may acquire a futile victory, but,

> If God is for us, who can be against us? He who did not spare His own Son, but delivered Him up for us all, how shall He not with Him also freely give us all things? Who shall bring a charge against God's elect? It is God who justifies. Who is he who condemns? It is Christ who died, and furthermore is also risen, who is even at the right hand of God, who also makes intercession for us. Who shall separate us from the love of Christ? Shall tribulation, or

distress, or persecution, or famine, or nakedness, or peril, or sword? (Rom. 8:31–35 NKJV)

God could give no greater sacrifice to atone for the sins of man than the sacrifice of His own Son! Our redemption demanded full recompense for our iniquities! He paid the sin debt for all eternity! Indeed, how shall He not with Him also freely give us all things (Rom. 8:32 NKJV)?

When we know His thoughts are forever for our good, then keeping His commands and maintaining an intimate relationship with Him is not burdensome but rewarding. Our earthly trials prove only to anchor our faith in His faithfulness. He bathes us in His Word, reenforcing us with His promises as He comforts us with His Holy Spirit, who leads and guides us into truth. Having an intimate relationship with the Father is no longer a religious duty or spiritual exercise; we enjoy being with each other as He humbly descends to our personal existence and caresses us with His presence. Jesus treasured His Father's presence more than his own life, and His affection drove him to do the Father's will, no matter the cost. We, too, can lovingly obey Yehovah's commands as we learn to trust in His unseen hand. We will discover He is the most rewarding and greatest treasure ever!

> "If you love Me, keep My commandments. And I will pray the Father, and He will give you another Helper, that He may abide with you forever—the Spirit of truth, whom the world cannot receive, because it neither sees Him nor knows Him; but you know Him, for He dwells with you and will be in you. I will not leave you orphans; I will come to you." (John 14:15–18 NKJV)

This is the Father's daily commune with His children. He sees and loves us through His Holy Spirit. The Comforter will lead and guide us in the right path to go and keep our feet from stumbling. And so that is where we live. It is not because we are perfect in all that we do and say; it is that we have struggled, endured tribulation, and learned to trust His faithfulness, even if we often fail. When we cry out in our despair, He hears us and brings us through the other side. Though it may not be on our perceived timetable, we learn to trust.

Do not give up on your Savior! Keep trusting in the Lord. Things will be tough through life. Some people will be hard-hearted, and others will be judgmental, but we must protect our hearts and be willing to forgive, to bless and curse not. Trials are allowed by Yehovah to enhance our resolve, to clarify our position, and to strengthen us through adversity. Yehovah will use trials, tribulation, and rejection to remind you of what you are forsaking, of whose you are becoming, and to walk humbly before Him. We consecrate our lives to serve Him. Whether or not others accept our new life is irrelevant.

Peter once proclaimed that he was willing to suffer for the Lord:

> Simon Peter said to Him, "Lord, where are You going?" Jesus answered him, "Where I am going you cannot follow Me now, but you shall follow Me afterward." Peter said to Him, "Lord, why can I not follow You now? I will lay down my life for Your sake." (John 13: 36–38 NKJV)

Peter did not know that Jesus was speaking of His impending crucifixion and Peter's eventual crucifixion. This type of prophecy is seldom heard in modern-day Christian circles. Who could bear it? Who would dare proclaim such a negative, antiprosperity message? It would require the continual abiding power of the Holy Spirit to keep Simon Peter on course throughout his ministry.

> And the Lord said, "Simon, Simon, behold, Satan hath desired to have you, that he may sift you as wheat: But I have prayed for thee, that thy faith fail not: and when thou art converted, strengthen thy brethren." (Luke 22:31–32 NKJV)

Our beloved Simon had stuck his ambition right in the middle of the fires of tribulation.

After the Last Supper, Simon Peter would deny the Lord Jesus three times. Even after being forewarned by Jesus, Peter missed it again terribly. Now Peter is enduring crushing guilt, desperate for hope, condemned, a failure, a liar, a deserter, and a denier. Surely, if there was ever a candidate to give up on, it was Peter. I think most of us would have assessed the situation as dire and beyond reconciliation, but Jesus's love is greater than our weakness. He never lost a single sheep except the son of perdition. Even Judas Iscariot was one sheep too many. I cannot fathom the loss that Jesus must have felt even for the one who betrayed Him. Some things we cannot know, but the love of the Savior is without measure and captures the soul of those who love Him. Jesus knew the frailty of Peter, just as He knows our frailties and desperate need for redemption; we are beyond saving ourselves. It took the righteous blood of the Son of Yehovah to purchase our redemption, the obedience of a loving Savior to do His Father's will.

Maybe you have been in a desperate place like Peter. Have you ever been weakened by circumstances, incurred a serious illness, surrounded by fear and struggling just to breathe, wondering where your faith went? Poverty covers your faith. The darkness is overbearing and bewildering as you wonder, *What happened to His promises? Did I lose them? Can my faith be found again?* Let us see what Jesus does next.

Peter denied his Lord after having witnessed innumerable miracles. Now he was left to his own thoughts and mountains of grief and condemnation. So what does Peter do? He does what most men do when they have no answers; they go back to whatever they were before, same old Peter, same old fisherman. But Jesus does not stop loving Peter. He does not condemn His disciple for his failure. After His resurrection, Jesus finds Peter fishing on the Sea of Galilee (Tiberius) and calls to them, "Children, have you any food?" (John 21:5 NKJV). Absent any malice or hatred, Jesus was compassionately pursuing Peter! With their ambition lost, what "food" were they pursuing? Whose will were they seeking?

We see the true character of Jesus as he draws His children to himself without judgment. He calls to them, and then He blesses them with a bountiful catch. He has a fire of coals readied to cook them breakfast. Preparations made, He entreats them again, "Come and eat breakfast" (John 21:12 NKJV). There is no wrath in His voice, though none of them dared ask who He was, for they knew it was Jesus. They were caught unawares, fishing. Here is their Messiah, humbly teaching, feeding, and comforting His children. Christ's compassion encompasses their souls; here, once again, is the Savior they know and love.

After breakfast, Jesus asked Simon Peter if he loved (*agapao*) Him dearly. "Simon, son of Jonah, do you love Me more than these?" (John 21:15b NKJV), as from the heart, as with all the attributes Christ demonstrated in His ministry. Peter replies that he loved (*phileo*) Jesus more like a friend, someone likeable, someone you enjoy hanging around. Peter does not sugarcoat his response. He knows Jesus can spot a liar. He had seen Jesus cast out many demons over the course of their relationship. Then Jesus asked Peter the same question a second time, using the same word, agapao, the God kind of love. "Simon, son of Jonah, do you love Me?" (John 21:16 NKJV). Peter repeated his token friendship (phileo). Then, a third time, Jesus asks a different question, "Simon, son of Jonah, do you love Me?" (John 21:17 NKJV). This time, Jesus switched the word from agapao to phileo. Peter became grieved because Jesus changed the question from agapao to phileo. Peter became aware of his lack of devotion. Peter honestly assesses his inability to love with the same measure as Christ, or to lay down his life as Jesus had done, or that he loves the Lord more than his fellow disciples. Peter is caught between his own boastful profession and the reality that his love is no greater than his contemporaries. Satan had seized upon Peter's prideful statement. Jesus, of course, understood this from the beginning and forewarned Peter that Satan had sought to sift him like wheat. Despite Peter's bravado, Jesus loved him and prayed for his conversion, a transformation from a man of impulsivity to one of a faithful servant.

Follow Me

Peter's willingness and honesty to serve Jesus with only his phileo, or brotherly love, was good enough for Jesus. Jesus knew Peter's brokenness, his frailty, his denial, but more importantly, Jesus knew that Peter loved Him and that Peter's love would grow into agapao, the Yehovah type of love where we love others as much as we do ourselves, even our enemies. See Matthew 22:37, Luke 11:37, Romans 8:28, 1 Corinthians 8:3, 1 Peter 1:8, and 1 John 4:21.

Peter's Christlikeness grew through every triumph and failure; he was learning what agapao love was as he followed the Master. Jesus never ceased pouring His affection and grace into Peter, just as He continues to pour

Himself into all those who love Him. He is a faithful Redeemer, merciful and patient, worthy of our love and relentless affection.

As if that lesson were not enough, after Christ corrected Peter,

> Then Peter, turning around, saw the disciple whom Jesus loved following, who also had leaned on His breast at the supper, and said, "Lord, who is the one who betrays You?" Peter, seeing him, said to Jesus, "But Lord, what about this man?" (John 21:20–21 NKJV)

Peter's mind began to wander after having just been corrected. He considered his position as being Christ's servant and that he was not greater than his fellow disciples and certainly not greater than Jesus. Peter wondered, would the cross be required of him as well? As Yeshua had said,

> Most assuredly, I say to you, a servant is not greater than his master; nor is he who is sent greater than he who sent him. (John 13:16 NKJV)

While reflecting on the cross that he had seen Jesus endure, Peter recalls Jesus's foretelling of his denial.

> And the Lord said, "Simon, Simon! Indeed, Satan has asked for you, that he may sift you as wheat." (Luke 22:31 NKJV)

Peter must have been reeling from the prospect that the cross would be his eventual outcome, too, and it explains why he later fled at Jesus's trial. Presently, however, this made him anxious and envious of the one who leaned his head on Jesus's breast.

> Peter, seeing him, said to Jesus, "But Lord, what about this man?" Jesus said to him, "If I will that he remain till I come, what is that to you? You follow Me." (John 21:21–22 NKJV)

Jesus was teaching Peter again. Jesus did not attempt to assuage Peter's fear. There was no prosperity message of riches and promises of soft living; it was an intentional reminder to consider his option of obedience or self-will. Often, our personal ambitions, difficult circumstances, and hard charges require direct communication. "You follow Me." Jesus fully intended for Simon Peter to get the message. "It is none of your business what My other servants do. Do you want to do what I want you to do, or do want to do your own will?"

> "If you love Me, you will keep My commandments." (John 14:15 ESV) (love = agapao)

Recall that Satan wanted to sift Peter as wheat; he is still sifting the saints of God. We are at war with darkness. It was not a question whether Jesus loved Peter; it was a matter of keeping Peter's feet on the path that Jesus laid before him. This instruction was not hard-hearted; it was filled with compassion and protection for Peter. The question to us today is equally revealing. Do we trust the Lord's love for us personally? Do we accept that He is actively engaged in promoting His perfect will through us for our own good, our own protection, though it may cost us everything? Or are we merely interested in Him prospering our life or agenda? Discerning the truth of these questions is key to understanding the degree of our faith, maturity, and relationship with the Father. And if your assessment finds you lacking in devotion to do the Father's will (join the club), be honest. Be like Peter. Complain about it to Jesus. Take your correction and keep following the Savior. His grace is sufficient for you too (2 Cor. 12:9)!

No greater love hath a man, or a Savior, than to lay down their life for their neighbor. Like Peter, we cannot now fathom the love that the Father has bestowed upon us through Jesus Christ, but as we grow and give our lives to Him, we too will be converted and, one day soon, rejoice with exceeding joy in His presence (Jude 1:24).

Going back to just after the Last Supper, they were praying in the Garden of Gethsemane. Luke 22:40 (NKJV) says, "When He came to the place, He said to them, 'Pray that you may not enter into temptation.'" They had just eaten. It was dark. It had been a long day, so what did they do? They all fell asleep. None of them stayed to pray with Jesus. Later, they all deserted Him during His trials, and Peter fulfilled the prophecy of denying the Lord Jesus three times. That is a tough lesson. All too often, we do the same thing. We get comfortable with our Lord and then neglect our service to Him. Jesus told them,

> "Pray that you may not enter into temptation." (Luke 22:40 NKJV)

> It is also part of the Lord's Prayer:
> "And do not lead us into temptation." (Matt. 6:13 NKJV)

> That is to say, don't allow me to fall because of my weakness.
> "But deliver us from the evil one." (Matt. 6:13 NKJV)

We must remain steadfast, fight the good fight daily, and be watchful in prayer for ourselves and for our neighbor.

> Harsh discipline is for him who forsakes the way, And he who hates correction will die. (Prov. 15:10 NKJV)

Peter had issues to work through, as we all do. The Holy Spirit will convict, comfort, and strengthen us as we overcome all our obstacles. Yehovah is faithful, and training us to be faithful is a labor of love for Him. He has all the answers, all the power, all the ability to recreate us. We have the choice of whom we will serve. Will you keep your hand to the plow? I encourage you not to give up on the task of developing Yeshua's character in your life! It is not easy. It is not cheap. It is not every person's desire to be one whose heart is surrendered to the Father. We choose daily, one way or the other. We are walking in a dual reality, citizens of earth and citizens of heaven. Our life choices decide eternal consequences. Do not let the slick world deceive you. Our prayer warfare will keep us from falling into temptation (Luke 22:40).

There are many tricks out there, and we, like sheep, are not capable of seeing them, avoiding, and overcoming them alone. We must follow the Shepherd. Listen to His voice. Follow the leading of the Holy Spirit. He will not be flamboyant. He will not be prideful. He will not lie or deceive. He is always tender, always merciful. He will grant you wisdom and knowledge as you listen to His voice. And remember,

> But the wisdom that is from above is first pure, then peaceable, gentle, willing to yield, full of mercy and good fruits, without partiality and without hypocrisy. (James 3:17 NKJV)

CHAPTER 12

FISH AND CHIPS, OR WHY DO WE FOLLOW JESUS?

I used to think that the Gospel of Jesus Christ was simple. I like simplicity, but that is apparently only for the youthful, as somehow the Word of God's breadth and depth seem to grow the more I read it. Similarly, the Mosaic Covenant proves to be quite different with its in-depth instructions, observances, and commandments; it requires a lifetime of study. Many read the Pentateuch (the first five books of the Old Testament), observe its detailed instructions, and get lost in the weeds, trying to wade their way through it all. It must have been the straightforward weed picker instructions my mom taught me when I was young. She would say, "Grab them deep, down by the root, squeeze tight, and pull the whole thing out all at once. That ensures it will not grow back." I usually use that metaphor when discussing how to deal with sin, but somehow it has leeched over here into searching out scriptures, seeking the truth of them; it, too, is a lot like pulling those weeds. If what the Lord is instructing me gets too complicated to understand, I sometimes slack off a bit, snapping the weed at the surface, allowing it to grow back again. Sin does that too; it will keep coming back at you. Fortunately, the Holy Spirit prods and pulls until eventually I find myself back over there tugging for the answer. Father created us as gardeners. We are now digging to learn what once was given freely. I ask myself, "Where has the simplicity gone in serving Jesus that I knew in my youth?" In addition to the Mosaic

Covenant, we have become bombarded with extrabiblical New Covenant doctrinal dogma, duties, and prohibitions that are not a part of the Gospel of Jesus Christ. We need to remember that Yeshua said,

> "Come to Me, all you who labor and are heavy laden, and I will give you rest. Take My yoke upon you and learn from Me, for I am gentle and lowly in heart, and you will find rest for your souls. For My yoke is easy and My burden is light." (Matt. 11:28–30 NKJV)

When we take our eyes off the Savior's teaching and focus on man's precepts, then following Jesus becomes confusing. We become distraught and frustrated and grow apathetic. Let's not lose sight of our Lord's yoke, His gentleness and humility.

The Word of Yehovah is awesome, teeming with knowledge, revelation, wisdom, and intrigue. For simpleminded persons as myself, I need things explained in depth, repeatedly, in a straightforward manner. Oddly, Yehovah has so arranged the Word of Yehovah that it is not presented in chronological order. The narrative jumps around quite a bit between different books and authors; piecing it all together takes diligence and honest introspection, without which you will never unravel its mysteries. You must have the help of the Holy Spirit to unfold them. Often there are truths strewn throughout its books that require significant effort to glean, while other truths appear without effort.

> Ask, and it will be given to you; seek, and you will find; knock, and it will be opened to you. (Matt. 7:7 NKJV)

Among the confusion, let us not lose sight of the simplicity that is Christ (2 Cor. 11:3). If we are sincere in our study of Yehovah's Word, the Holy Spirit will be our teacher, guiding us with His unseen hand, revealing Yehovah's wisdom and peaceful instruction.

The book of Micah is largely a forewarning of destruction, yet within its short narrative is Yehovah's simple instruction toward repentance. It contains the prophet Micah's instruction for a good life. It is simple, direct, and easily understood.

> He has shown you, O man, what is good; And what does
> the Lord require of you But to do justly, To love mercy, And
> to walk humbly with your God? (Mic. 6:8 NKJV)

Micah feared the Lord and prophesied of the destruction of Samaria and Jerusalem because of their sin. He knew the character of Yehovah and trusted in His mercy. He understood the Law's function and forewarned the people of their impending destruction with the intention of bringing them to repentance and avoiding captivity. Even while prophesying the harshest of criticisms, Micah did not lose focus of the heart of God and how the Law was given to bring about righteousness and restore man back to the Father. Unfortunately, the people did not repent and seek the Lord. Their destruction and captivity were done by their own hand, much like today's world. A love for Yeshua remains our bread of life.

King David is another messianic type who loved Yehovah from his youth. He knew the heart of Yehovah as one of holiness, protection, unselfish love, and a fierce devotion for His people, Israel. King David never lost his trust in Yehovah's mercy, even through all his triumphs and his sin. It was a simple devotion, wholly leaning on the Father's goodness and mercy. During David's flight from King Saul, when the king was trying to kill David, he ran through the temple and took the showbread that rested before the holy of holies, bread intended only for Yehovah and then given to the priests (Matt. 12:4). The showbread symbolized the bread of life who was to come down from heaven, likened to the manna in the wilderness. This bread showed forth the body of Christ that was to be given for mankind, from Bethlehem, which means House of Bread. Bethlehem was only a few miles away, south of Jerusalem, and would one day bring forth the Messiah. David's faith was in the coming Redeemer, the giver of life. His faith transcended the Law of Moses, which prohibited him and his men from taking the showbread. David's faith rested in the promised Messiah and the New Covenant (Jer. 31:31).

Jesus stated in John 4:34,

> "My food is to do the will of Him who sent Me, and to
> finish His work." (John 4:34 NKJV)

He was partaking of the Spirit of Life, which he received from Yehovah, where God's Holy Spirit speaks to spirit, deep speaks to deep, and heavenly discourse is the spiritual nourishment of purpose and being. Our Messiah was driven by his affection for the Father, inseparable and indiscernible one from the other. Jesus's motivation to suffer a humiliating and cruel death was not based on duty or command but on absolute trust, love, and oneness with the Father. Jesus would not be deterred; his life, his purpose, his bread was to do the Father's will. It was Yehovah's Word manifest in flesh that died on that cross, not a mere human being but the express image, nature, and character of the Father in human form. Jesus knew Yehovah better than any of us and allowed Himself to be sacrificed to extend that fellowship to all who would believe in Him. We are invited to know the Father as intimately as the Son knows Him! To love Him with all our heart, soul, mind, and strength.

Surely, our food is the same as He who created us. So where are we, His children, to buy this food? Certainly not in the Sea of Galilee. What work has He laid out for us to complete? Fortunately, it is not too difficult to find or to do.

> Then they said to Him, "What shall we do, that we may work the works of God?" Jesus answered and said to them, "This is the work of God, that you believe in Him whom He sent." (John 6:28–29 NKJV)

Our work, therefore, is to trust in who Yeshua Hamashiach is, what He said, and what He did on our behalf. Our old sin nature inhibited us from keeping the Old Testament Law, but He has determined a new nature for those who love Him by giving us of his own nature, a New Covenant, and a work of faith that we too can engage, the same work that Abraham did—"believe in Him."

CHAPTER 13

WHAT IS THE SABBATH REST AND HOW DO WE ENTER HIS REST?

As we walk with the Lord, taking on His nature and expelling our old life, we grow to learn that the meaning of rest is to cease from our futile way of life, our striving to reach perfection by keeping commandments. We learn to trust in the Father's Spirit of Life in Christ Jesus.

> For the Gentiles shall seek Him, And His resting place
> shall be glorious. (Isa. 11:10 NKJV)

Let us examine for a moment the similarities between the children of Israel, who refused to enter the Promised Land with Moses and Joshua, and the New Covenant promise of our Lord's eternal Sabbath rest.

In reference to the Hebrew children who refused to enter the Promised land, Paul writes,

> For who, having heard, rebelled? Indeed, was it not all who
> came out of Egypt, led by Moses? Now with whom was He
> angry forty years? Was it not with those who sinned, whose
> corpses fell in the wilderness? And to whom did He swear

that they would not enter His rest, but to those who did
not obey? So, we see that they could not enter in because
of unbelief. (Heb. 3:16–19 NKJV)

See also Hebrews 3:8–11.

Though this application may seem obscure, the object lesson is that
when the Father provides an opportunity and promises to provide safe
passage, after He has already provided your deliverance with mighty
miracles from Egyptian bondage (read as bondage to the Law), it would be
a wise decision to move into the blessings ahead (read as New Covenant).
Yehovah never intends evil for His children.

God is light and in Him is no darkness at all. (1 John 1:5
NKJV)

Do we have faith to move from the religious trappings based on the
Law of Moses into the mercy of Yehovah? To trust and be nourished by
the Spirit of Life flowing from His throne and to rest in His presence
versus ceaselessly striving to attain perfection based on our own merits? In
Hebrews 3:12, Paul is writing to those of the Jewish faith:

Beware, brethren, lest there be in any of you an evil heart
of unbelief in departing from the living God. (Heb. 3:12
NKJV)

For the children of Israel, it was primary and essential that they did
not forsake their confidence in Yeshua Hamashiach, their newly revealed
Messiah. It's another stern warning to the Messianic Hebrew and the
Gentile Christian to enter in and not to turn back to the Mosaic Law. Paul
reiterates this warning in his letter again in Hebrews 4:2,

For indeed the gospel was preached to us as well as to
them; but the word which they heard did not profit them,
not being mixed with faith in those who heard it. (Heb.
4:2 NKJV)

If we don't receive the limitless grace and mercy God provisioned for us in the Good News of Jesus Christ, there is nothing greater that He can offer than His own Son.

> Then God blessed the seventh day and sanctified it, because in it He rested from all His work which God had created and made. (Gen. 2:3 NKJV)

Here, we can see that the day in which Yehovah rested is not explicitly given as a commandment to Adam to rest on the seventh day, neither in the garden before the Fall nor after the Fall. The Law of the Sabbath did not come until Moses at Mt. Sinai. Did Yehovah forget to mention it as a commandment to Adam, or did Moses forget to write it down? Did any of the forefathers preceding Moses observe the seventh day? Are we missing some yet to be discovered historical text? Did Yehovah mention the sanctity of the seventh day in His discourses with Adam before the Fall? I think God shared many things with Adam with much greater ease than He can communicate to us today. Either way, we are blessed to have the seventh day as a marker to remind us to rest in our Father's provision. Yehovah made it for us. Why shouldn't we partake of it? Or is there a greater purpose?

After the children of Israel are delivered from Egypt and before Yehovah initiates the Mosaic Covenant, He addresses the Sabbath for the first time to the children of Israel, approximately forty-five days after they left Egypt (Exod. 16:1). Then in Exodus 16:23,

> Then he said to them, "This is what the Lord has said: 'Tomorrow is a Sabbath rest, a holy Sabbath to the Lord." (Exod. 16:23 NKJV)

The Hebrew children had not kept the Sabbath. Either by neglect or by ignorance, they knew little of the Sabbath and its gift to mankind. Then, later in Exodus 31:14,

> "You shall keep the Sabbath, therefore, for it is holy to you. Everyone who profanes it shall surely be put to death; for

whoever does any work on it, that person shall be cut off from among his people." (Exod. 31:14 NKJV)

Now, upon the giving of the Mosaic Covenant, breaking the Sabbath resulted in being excommunicated, cut off from the assembly of Israel, an outcast who would be denied access to Yehovah's salvation. Whether they previously knew of the Sabbath or not, it now became a deadly offense! That is a surefire method of maintaining compliance. This must be where today's overzealous preachers get the idea to blast the local congregation to keep the Lord's Day, as I've heard it preached with almost as much dire consequence. Fear is a good motivator, but without love, it's just another religious exercise that diminishes one's trust in a loving God.

> You made known to them Your holy Sabbath, and commanded them precepts, statutes and laws, By the hand of Moses Your servant. (Neh. 9:14 NKJV)

Did they not know of the Sabbath before Yehovah made it known to them through Moses? Nehemiah clearly states that Moses made it known to them, which implies that they did not previously know of the Sabbath (Deut. 5:2–3). Though not specifically addressed in our canonized Bible, there are many references implying the patriarchs taught their descendants the laws of God and to keep His commands, though none specifically address the seventh day or the Sabbath. As the seventh day was important to Yehovah to sanctify it, He most likely informed them about sanctifying the seventh day but not necessarily as the Sabbath that Moses taught. Additionally, there are extrabiblical texts, such as the book of Jubilees, that substantiate the observance of the Sabbath after Moses but not prior to. I believe they had the seventh day handed down to them from their forefathers ever since the days of Adam, but not the Sabbath covenant as given to Moses. The Mosaic Covenant underscored the holy day as now being mandatory—written into a binding life-or-death covenant! The children of Israel would no longer be traveling or working on the Sabbath. There would be no industry or business conducted that day, as they were instructed to prepare their meals the day before so as not to even cook on the Sabbath. It is quite the contrast to the dictums imposed by the modern Lord's Day observance (first day of the week, being Sunday, a Pagan reference to the sun god), when so many Christians are subjected to peer pressure, hurried, frantic, irritable, and wearied, getting to church to play musical chairs. I believe we have missed the point.

As we go through this journey of religious observances, it will appear that the pendulum will swing to and fro between the Sabbath and the Lord's Day. My research certainly had me swinging between the two, questioning my convictions, frustrated and bouncing from one set of very convincing arguments to another. In retrospect, I am grateful to have been run through the mill. The shell of my convictions was cracked away, that only the truth of Messiah's Sabbath would remain my security and give me resounding peace.

So, which example are we to follow, the Sabbath or the Lord's Day? Or has the Sabbath's rest been transformed into something else?

Once again, we must remember that the Gentile Christian was never under the Mosaic Covenant, and as such, there is not a specific commandment for the Messianic Hebrew or Christian to observe the Sabbath as defined in the Mosaic Covenant. There is a lot of spirited debate about this subject. I think God intended it to be this way. Why? Because until the child of God earnestly seeks to know the truth, truth will remain of little consequence to them. But in the day the child of God desires to know God's redemptive plan, they will subject themselves to the work of extracting the truth of the matter. And once that is done, they will recognize the utter hopelessness of being justified by the works of the Law, a disappointing acknowledgment of our desperate condition. That, my friend, is precisely where Yehovah wants us—standing at His feet, completely incapable, desiring our nakedness to be clothed. The Good News of the Gospel of Jesus Christ is exceedingly gracious and full of mercy. It's the only way He could save us. He has paid our sin debt and covers our nakedness with His robe of righteousness. Not because we deserve it but simply because Yehovah loves us and desires not to condemn us (John 3:16–17)!

As we move further into this topic, keep in mind that the Sabbath was created for mankind (Mark 2:27), not God. It is Yehovah's intention to provide eternal rest for His children. The mechanisms He employed to go about bringing in that rest were constructed to focus our hearts away from our weaknesses and to look upon the Savior who died for us. Spoiler alert! Yeshua Hamashiach, as Lord of the Sabbath (Matt. 12:8, Mark 2:28, Luke

6:5) created, kept, and replaced the temporary Sabbath as contained in the Mosaic Covenant with His own life. He has become our eternal Sabbath rest. This is the purpose behind Father sanctifying the seventh day in Genesis 2:3. He created it to foreshadow our redemption! However, the Father never rescinded the day of rest that He set aside for humanity. The seventh day is still the last day of the week; we do not have a six-day week. Father wisely added to the seventh day our Savior's perpetual atonement. You may ask, "So what is our obligation to observe the Sabbath since Christ Jesus has become our Sabbath?" It is to walk in the liberty to be free from the legal requirement as contained within the Mosaic Law and the liberty to rejoice, take leisure, and commune with Yeshua and the Father. We still need physical, mental, and spiritual rest in the Holy Spirit. We need not allow the enemy to trip us up with condemnation about the Sabbath, as Romans 8:1 shows how God already completed this requirement for us.

> For what the law could not do in that it was weak through
> the flesh, God did by sending His own Son in the likeness
> of sinful flesh, on account of sin: He condemned sin in the
> flesh, that the righteous requirement of the law might be
> fulfilled in us who do not walk according to the flesh but
> according to the Spirit. (Rom. 8:3–4 NKJV)

God did is the operative phrase here. Rest in what Christ Jesus did for you, and you will be blessed.

Surprisingly, there is no specific command or scripture to observe the lawful Sabbath or the Lord's Day in the New Covenant, except as provisioned within Yeshua Hamashiach as our Sabbath rest. We have simply followed the tradition of our ancestors in observing the first day of the week (Sunday). Though the early church did come together on the first day of the week, it was simply accepted since Yeshua Hamashiach appeared to the apostles on that day. It certainly seems plausible and a great reason to observe the first day of the week, but again, there is no commandment to do so; thus we are at liberty to observe both the Sabbath and the Lord's Day, if desired. Of course, it is in our best interest to routinely fellowship with other believers, to observe the Lord's Supper and study scriptures. It is my humble opinion that either of these days appears to be sufficient, as do the remaining five, to rest in Christ Jesus. The important thing is to rest in Yeshua, fellowship, and celebrate our Savior's gift of salvation and eternal life together. We need to encourage one another and continue to work toward developing the unity of the body of Christ every day. But let's examine the scriptures further.

Sabbath Day's Confusion

Many modern-day Christians observe the Lord's Day, the first day of the week, as the day Yeshua was raised from the dead. However, Yeshua did not rise on a Sunday morning but on the evening of the prior day, on the Sabbath Day. It's a bit difficult to track on the Hebrew calendar, as their days are numbered differently, based on a 364-day-per-year cycle. And to make it more confusing, we need to understand that the Hebrews do not count their days beginning at midnight, like most cultures do today, but as beginning and ending at dusk of each afternoon. As soon as the sun sets, it is the next day.

As we go through this subject, remember that the seventh day existed from the first week of creation in Genesis long before the Mosaic Covenant's Sabbath, and the two are distinctly different in their application. So, to follow this chain of events, we must go back to the Exodus account when the Hebrew children made preparation to observe the first Passover event in Egypt. We read the instructions regarding the Passover lamb, or goat, in Exodus 12:6:

> "Now you shall keep it until the fourteenth day of the same
> month. Then the whole assembly of the congregation of
> Israel shall kill it at twilight." (Exod. 12:6 NKJV)

That is, during the first month of the Hebrew calendar, the month of Nisan, count fourteen days and kill the sacrificial lamb at twilight, meaning at dusk, before dark. The Egyptian exiles were commanded to roast the Passover lamb at twilight and then eat the Passover lamb through the night.

> "Then they shall eat the flesh on that night; roasted in fire,
> with unleavened bread and with bitter herbs they shall eat
> it." (Exod. 12:8 NKJV)

The term *night* confirms the transition from day fourteen to day fifteen.

> "And thus you shall eat it: with a belt on your waist, your
> sandals on your feet, and your staff in your hand. So you
> shall eat it in haste. It is the Lord's Passover." (Exod. 12:11
> NKJV)

Later that night, while safely in their homes, the angel of death would *pass over* their homes, beginning at midnight, this being the fifteenth night of the first month of the Hebrew calendar. Again, the Hebrew calendar twenty-four-hour cycle begins at dark or sunset (Gen. 1:3–5), not at midnight and not in the morning. Also, the Hebrew calendar months are numbered one through twelve, with some years having thirteen months, and the new year begins in the spring, not winter. More on this later.

The Hebrew nation was given a very peculiar sign of the Messiah to come, one that would be impossible to miss. We find it in the book of Jonah:

> Now the Lord had prepared a great fish to swallow Jonah.
> And Jonah was in the belly of the fish three days and three
> nights. (Jonah 1:17 NKJV)

Jonah was sent as a reluctant prophet to witness to the heathen city of Ninevah, a pagan country that hated the Hebrew nation and committed horrific acts against the Hebrew people. Nonetheless, Yehovah had mercy on them because they lived in ignorance and were spiritually blind. It's a remarkable story of God's mercy and tenderness toward heathen idol worshippers and even to stubborn prophets.

Later in Yeshua's ministry, he referenced the miraculous resurrection of Jonah from the belly of a great fish to His own resurrection:

> An evil and adulterous generation seeks after a sign, and
> no sign will be given to it except the sign of the prophet
> Jonah. For as Jonah was three days and three nights in the
> belly of the great fish, so will the Son of Man be three days
> and three nights in the heart of the earth. (Matt. 12:39–40
> NKJV)

Yeshua, like Jonah, was sent to preach deliverance to the ignorant and spiritually blind Hebrew first, and later to the Gentiles through the apostles.

Multiple Sabbaths

It is important to understand that there were fifty-two seventh-day Sabbaths (Saturdays) throughout the Hebrew year, but there are also seven more high holy day observances that are also called Sabbaths, days where no work could be performed. We find all of them detailed in Leviticus, chapter 23, as the following:

1. Seventh-day Sabbath, fifty-two per year, and referred to by Gentiles as Saturday
2. Lord's Passover (Pesach), day of Yeshua's crucifixion, occurs in the first month of the Hebrew calendar, on the fourteenth day of Nisan (or Aviv)
3. Feast of Unleavened Bread, occurs on 15–21 Nisan
4. Feast of First Fruits, occurs on the seventh-day Sabbath following the Passover Sabbath
5. Feast of Weeks, ends fifty days after the Feast of First Fruits, also known as Pentecost
6. Feast of Trumpets, occurs on the first day of the seventh month, Tishri
7. Day of Atonement, occurs on the tenth day of Tishri
8. Feast of Tabernacles, occurs on the fifteenth day of Tishri

The day of Passover also began the week of the Feast of Unleavened Bread. There is an assembly, a convocation, on the first day and the seventh day of the Feast of Unleavened Bread.

> "On the first day there shall be a holy convocation, and on the seventh day there shall be a holy convocation for you. No manner of work shall be done on them; but that which everyone must eat—that only may be prepared by you." (Exod. 12:16 NKJV)

In our modern translations, the term *Feast of Unleavened Bread* is sometimes referred to as a Sabbath or a high holy day. The Feast of Unleavened Bread is a Sabbath week, which makes it a bit confusing to follow. Therefore, I will use these terms to distinguish between the three holy observations: Passover, Feast of Unleavened Bread, and the weekly seventh day.

The Lord's Passover

> On the fourteenth day of the first month at twilight is the Lord's Passover. (Lev. 23:5 NKJV)

The first observance, Passover, occurs in Exodus 12:6, Leviticus 23:5, and Ezekiel 45:21. The preparation of the lamb was done the fourteenth day of Nisan and was performed in the late evening, before night. The eating of the lamb or goat was done immediately at the conclusion of the twilight of the fourteenth of Nisan. After roasting the lamb in darkness, it would be the fifteenth of Nisan (reference Genesis 1:5 for Yehovah's definition of a day). The Lord's Passover occurred on the fourteenth of Nisan, but the Passover meal was eaten on the fifteenth of Nisan when the Feast of Unleavened Bread began and continued for seven days. Often, the two are combined and referred to as Passover, the Passover week, or the Feast of Unleavened Bread, and last for a total of seven days.

Yeshua observed Passover with His disciples at the beginning of the fourteenth of Nisan and was crucified later that same day in the late evening of the fourteenth of Nisan.

> Now when evening had come, because it was the Preparation Day, that is, the day before the Sabbath. (Mark 15:42)

The Feast of Unleavened Bread, is what is being referred to by Joseph of Arimathea and Nicodemus to Pilate when they requested the body of Jesus to be taken down before the Sabbath. See also Luke 23:50–52 and John 19:31.

The Hebrew children did not observe the eating of the lamb until nighttime, the fifteenth of Nisan. This begins the high holy day of the Feast of Unleavened Bread, where the first day there is a holy assembly, called a convocation.

The neglect to properly identify the Feast of Unleavened Bread as the Sabbath immediately following the Lord's Passover (Yeshua's crucifixion) has led many to believe that the Sabbath mentioned in Mark 15:42 was the seventh day, which it was not; it was the Feast of Unleavened Bread. Therefore, Mary and Mary Magdalene, after observing where Yeshua had been laid (Mark 15:47), departed to observe the Feast of Unleavened Bread. Thereafter, they observed another preparation day on the sixth day (Friday), for the upcoming seventh-day Sabbath (Saturday). This neglect has caused confusion with many, as the three days and three nights of Jonah's prophecy cannot possibly fit in with a crucifixion on Friday and a resurrection on Sunday.

Feast of Unleavened Bread

The second holy observance, also a Sabbath, was termed the Feast of Unleavened Bread. It is a feast of seven days that immediately follows the Lord's Passover, where they eat unleavened bread in memorial of their traveling out of Egypt in haste. There is a holy convocation (assembly) on the first day and another on the last day, when no labor can be performed except for the preparation of daily meals. Leaven is a metaphor for sin, or the pride of sin, as it enlarges itself and puffs one up. Cleansing ourselves from sin and pride is the Father's command, that He might dwell with us. This is analogous to the Hebrew children preparing for their exodus from bondage and baking unleavened bread. Yeshua Hamashiach, our Bread of Life, was arrested, beaten, scourged, and crucified on the day before the Feast of Unleavened Bread. The Feast of Unleavened Bread is the basis for what some refer to as Passover week, even though Passover is a one-day event.

> Now on the first day of the Feast of the Unleavened Bread the disciples came to Jesus, saying to Him, "Where do You want us to prepare for You to eat the Passover?" (Matt. 26:17 NKJV)

This scripture presents some challenges when compared to other Passover commandments, as the Feast of Unleavened Bread starts after the lamb is slain, as shown in Exodus 12:6, 15-17, Leviticus 23:5–6, and Ezekiel 45:21. Some scholars believe the disciples' statement in Matthew 26:17 alludes to the period of cleansing of the houses of leaven before Passover, days before the actual Feast of Unleavened Bread. I think it is a reasonable conclusion, as no work could be done during the feast, and leaven could not be present in the home or be in contact with anyone for the entire seven-day observance. Therefore, the leaven had to be extracted prior to the Feast of Unleavened Bread and most likely removed prior to the Passover of the fourteenth of Nisan. The disciples simply referred to both events collectively as preparatory time for the one-evening Passover and the following seven-day feast since they began together.

Seventh-Day Sabbath

The third holy observance occurring in what is often mistakenly called Passover week was the weekly seventh day, or normal Sabbath, which also had a preparation day on the sixth day of every week.

The Exodus of the children of Israel began the first day of the Feast of Unleavened Bread as they gathered the livestock and goods and plundered the distraught Egyptians of their silver, gold, and clothing, all while moving six hundred thousand men, their wives, and children out of Egypt (Exod. 12:37).

Let's look at a timeline as presented in the scriptures that will help us understand the actual events as they occurred.

+ Month 1 (Nisan), day 10, seventh day of the week, (Sabbath) – triumphal entry

> Now the Lord spoke to Moses and Aaron in the land of Egypt, saying, "This month shall be your beginning of months; it shall be the first month of the year to you. Speak to all the congregation of Israel, saying: 'On the tenth of this month every man shall take for himself a

lamb, according to the house of his father, a lamb for a household.'" (Exod. 12:3 NKJV)

- o This period of five days, from the tenth to the fourteenth day of Nisan, was given to allow inspection of the animal to ensure it was without spot, blemish, or sickness. It would be washed and tended daily, requiring intimate interaction with the sacrifice.
- o This act of selection and inspection corresponds to the triumphal entry day of the Messiah as He was being heralded about and proclaimed as king:

> On the tenth of this month every man shall take for himself a lamb. (Exod. 12:3 NKJV)

What a remarkable coincidence! As previously proven in scripture, this timeline does not support the Palm Sunday theory or the Good Friday theory.

- ✦ Month 1, day 14, preparation day (Wednesday)

> Now on the first day of the Feast of the Unleavened Bread the disciples came to Jesus, saying to Him, "Where do You want us to prepare for you to eat the Passover?" (Matt. 26:17 NKJV)

> Now on the first day of Unleavened Bread, when they killed the Passover lamb, His disciples said to Him, "Where do You want us to go and prepare, that You may eat the Passover?" (Mark 14:12 NKJV)

> Then came the Day of Unleavened Bread, when the Passover must be killed. And He sent Peter and John, saying, "Go and prepare the Passover for us, that we may eat." So they said to Him, "Where do You want us to prepare?" (Luke 22:7–9)

- The Feast of Unleavened Bread starts on the fifteenth of Nisan (Exod. 12:22). In Luke 22:7-9, the Passover and the feast are mentioned together though they are separate events. The disciples are making plans for both Sabbaths as they inquire as to where Jesus wanted them to prepare for them. They were merely referring to both events in a collective manner. The feast was at hand, not presently occurring but soon coming. If we look closely at the events that Yeshua blessed and shared with His disciples in Luke 22, Yeshua blesses and shares the wine and the bread. Some surmise that Yeshua did not have a paschal lamb at the dinner. I am convinced that He did. However, the more poignant part is that He did not mention it. Lamb was certainly a staple in the Hebrew diet, and excluding it from an early Passover observance would have been notable, as it still spoke of the Messiah, the Lamb of God to come. And here He is, presenting Himself before His disciples as He shares His body and His blood and begins to speak of His betrayal. The focus is not on the paschal lamb on the table but on the Lamb of God sitting before them (Luke 22:14–21).
- The Hebrew nation removed leaven from their houses before the Feast of Unleavened Bread (Exod. 12:15). As a precaution, it is presumed that the Hebrew children would sweep through their houses several days before the feast to remove all leaven, as the penalty for having any leaven in their bread or their homes or touching it was severe.
- The disciples' inquiry occurred during the day of the thirteenth of Nisan. They then made the preparations that same day, obtained the sacrificial lamb before twilight, sacrificed it, and roasted it for the supper later that night, the fourteenth of Nisan, when Jesus sat down with the twelve. Jesus, as Lord of the Sabbath, is supposedly observing the Passover a day early with His disciples, foretelling His sacrifice as the Lamb of God on this, His sacrificial day but the Hebrew's preparation day.

> So the disciples did as Jesus had directed them; and they prepared the Passover. When evening had come, He sat down with the twelve. (Matt. 26:19–20 NKJV)

- o Correspondingly, the Hebrew children in bondage in Egypt prepared for their departure on the day prior (the fourteenth of Nisan), then observed Passover after twilight, through the night (the fifteenth of Nisan), and then plundered the Egyptians in the morning and fled in haste that same day.
- o The disciples were preparing to observe the seven-day Feast of Unleavened Bread from the fifteenth day of the month of Abib (or Nisan) through the twenty-first day.

> "In the first month, on the fourteenth day of the month at evening, you shall eat unleavened bread, until the twenty-first day of the month at evening." (Exod. 12:18 NKJV)

The Paschal lamb (Passover) was eaten on the fifteenth of Nisan. However, Yeshua's Last Supper was eaten at evening, the beginning of the Fourteenth of Nisan. He would be crucified later that same day as the Lamb of God for the sins of the people.

> "Now you shall keep it until the fourteenth day of the same month. Then the whole assembly of the congregation of Israel shall kill it at twilight." (Exod. 12:6 NKJV)

- o After the Last Supper, at night, Yeshua was arrested in the Garden of Gethsemane, scourged, beaten through the night into the daylight, and crucified in the afternoon on the fourteenth of Nisan, then removed from the cross before sundown (Wednesday at twilight).

- They were allowed to keep the lamb only until the fourteenth of Nisan, so the Paschal lamb (Yeshua) had to be sacrificed prior to dusk, or it would have transgressed into the fifteenth of Nisan, Passover. The Passover meal began after dusk, at twilight, marking the beginning of the fifteenth of Nisan, and was eaten that night. There is a distinction here between the Lord's Passover and the first day of the Feast of Unleavened Bread. Yeshua observed the Lord's Passover both figuratively with His disciples and physically on the cross at Calvary on the fourteenth of Nisan.
- Yeshua Hamashiach, the firstborn son of Mary, was arrested, beaten, and crucified all on the fourteenth day of the first month (Nisan), the day before the Feast of Unleavened Bread, and the same day the Hebrew children in Egypt sacrificed their Passover lamb or goat at twilight. The Egyptian firstborn were slain that first Passover night, the fifteenth of Nisan (Exod. 12:12).
- Yeshua was kept in the belly of the earth until the afternoon of the seventeenth day of the first month, being Nisan (or Abib), just before dusk. This was done to fulfill the prophetic life of Jonah (Jonah 1:17, Matt. 12:40), three days and three nights in the belly of the fish (a metaphor for earth). As Messiah was crucified during the daylight of the fourteenth day of Nisan, His body could not remain unburied at dusk, since twilight began the high holy day, Feast of Unleavened Bread (the fifteenth of Nisan). Therefore, Yeshua was hurriedly buried before dusk (around 6:00 p.m.) on the fourteenth of Nisan (Wednesday). Then counting three full days and nights, Yeshua arose from the grave shortly before dusk on the seventeenth of Nisan, at the tail end of the weekly seventh-day Sabbath.

> So there they laid Jesus, because of the Jews' Preparation Day, for the tomb was nearby. (John 19:42 NKJV)

> Now when evening had come, because it was the Preparation Day, that is, the day before the

> Sabbath, Joseph of Arimathea, a prominent council member, who was himself waiting for the kingdom of God, coming and taking courage, went to Pilate and asked for the body of Jesus. (Mark 15:42–43)

o Jesus's body was taken down before a Sabbath, but what kind of Sabbath? In John 19:31, John also calls the day of Yeshua's crucifixion a preparation day, identifying it as a preceding day to a high holy day, the annual Feast of Unleavened Bread of the fifteenth of Nisan. This high holy Sabbath is an intermediate Sabbath, beginning with the Passover seder, and runs for seven days.

o Unbeknownst to the Pharisees, Sadducees, and Pilate, they had crucified the Lamb of God on the Lord's Passover around noon on the fourteenth of Nisan.

o After the Feast of Unleavened Bread of the fifteenth of Nisan, the fifth day of the week (Wednesday dusk to Thursday dusk), there would be another preparation day on the sixth day (Thursday dusk to Friday dusk) for the weekly seventh-day Sabbath. This sixth-day preparation day is mentioned in Luke 23:55–56 when the women saw where they laid Jesus in the tomb, and then they observed the Sabbath of the Feast of Unleavened Bread. These women are listed in Mark 15:47 as Mary Magdalene and Mary the mother of James, Joses, and Salome. Thereafter, on the sixth day, they probably gathered the burial spices, as they would have been unable to gather them on the next day, the weekly seventh-day Sabbath. After the seventh-day Sabbath, the women arrived at the tomb on the first day of the week before dawn (see Matthew 28:1, Mark 16:1–2).

> "After three days I will rise." (Matt. 27:63 NKJV)

Jesus was not in the tomb four nights but three. Counting Wednesday night through Friday night is three nights. A fourth night in the tomb would have been through Saturday night into Sunday at dawn.

- o When the women discovered the empty tomb, Jesus was already gone. Yeshua did not spend a fourth night in the tomb. It is mistaken to think that Yeshua rose from the dead on the first day of the week (Sunday). He was simply discovered the day after the Sabbath because the seventh-day Sabbath ended approximately twelve hours earlier, between twilight and nighttime the previous day.

- o As a recap, working our timeline from the seventh day as the day of Yeshua's resurrection, backward three days and three nights (Matt. 27:63) places us back on the fourth day of the week (Wednesday), the day of Yeshua's death, before dusk. Then, moving backward another four days would place us at the preceding seventh day of the week (Saturday) and the triumphal entry.

The scriptures and dates given above debase the practices of Palm Sunday, Yeshua's supposed resurrection on the first day of the week (Lord's Day), and the Good Friday crucifixion theories. None of these theories concur with the scriptures. Additionally, we in modern-day Christianity have ignored the sanctity of the seventh-day Sabbath, the additional seven high holy Sabbaths, and Yehovah's plan for our eternal rest in Yeshua Hamashiach. All the Lord's holy Sabbaths spoke of Yeshua Hamashiach, and their memorial observances continue to speak of Him.

Yeshua Hamashiach became our eternal atoning sacrifice on the fourth day of the week, Wednesday, the fourteenth of Nisan, the Lord's Passover. Though the Lord's Day title has become sacrosanct in modern days, Yeshua Hamashiach became our eternal Sabbath rest when He arose from the dead on the seventh-day Sabbath, the seventeenth of Nisan.

Calendar Dysfunction

The Hebrew calendar is based on a lunar timetable and is certainly confusing, as is the earlier Enochian calendar (see book of Jubilees, chapter 6), which is based on a different solar schedule with 364 days and not our customary 365, counting only 52 weeks x 7 = 364 days. To make up for each calendar's discrepancies, each calendar adjusts by adding days or months. This makes for some rather confusing date keeping when trying to transfer special holidays and dates between them. In the case of the Hebrew lunar calendar, each Hebrew month has different days allotted as compared to the Gregorian or Julian calendar. Its days vary from twenty-eight days, some with twenty-nine or thirty days. Additionally, there is a thirteenth month in the Hebrew calendar, occurring every few years as a self-correcting schedule. The Gregorian and Julian calendar calculations never coincide with the Hebrew calendar or its holy days.

Both the Gregorian and Julian calendars have their troubles as well. Each has added days to their construct of the typical 365-day year too (e.g., leap year). These calendars are imperfect. They do not coincide precisely with the other calendar models, and each requires tweaking to synchronize with the solar calendars as holy days are moved, number of days are added or deleted, and so on. So what happens when days are added to a year as compared to other calendar models? Numbered weeks, months, and special holy days on the Hebrew calendar are misaligned on the Gentile calendars. Without going into extensive detail in this book, a quick internet search or a study in the book of Maccabees, which details Yehovah's acceptable calendar year, will convince the reader that the Enochian and Hebrew calendars look nothing like our present-day calendar. Julian and Gregorian calendars are skewed considerably when compared to biblical calendars. This is of little importance to the pagan but is of immense importance to keeping God's timetable of holy observances accurately.

As we know from the four Gospels (Matt. 27, Mark 15, Luke 23, John 19:31), Yeshua Hamashiach was crucified, died, then taken down from the cross. As it was the preparation day before a high Sabbath day, the Feast of Unleavened Bread, they hurriedly placed Christ's body in the tomb of Joseph of Arimathea.

> Therefore, because it was the Preparation Day, that the bodies should not remain on the cross on the Sabbath (for that Sabbath was a high day). (John 19:31 NKJV)

> Now when evening had come, because it was the Preparation Day, that is, the day before the Sabbath,

Joseph of Arimathea, a prominent council member, who was himself waiting for the kingdom of God, coming and taking courage, went in to Pilate and asked for the body of Jesus. (Mark 15:42 NKJV)

Some desire to honor Yeshua Hamashiach on the first day of the week because that is when Mary and the women first discovered that He had risen from the dead. Mary didn't witness Yeshua rise from the dead but merely found an empty tomb. Apparently, Yeshua rose from the dead after three days and nights and went to set the captives free in Abraham's bosom (Eph. 4:8). Now, we customarily call it the Lord's Day, though it is a bit misleading since He didn't rise from the dead on the first day, Sunday, but on the seventh day. And Good Friday never happened, as Yeshua was not crucified on a Friday. Despite these issues, we are at liberty to honor Yeshua Hamashiach on the first day of the week as the Lord's Day, and for some other good reasons:

1. Messiah's empty tomb was discovered on the first day of the week.
2. He appeared to the apostles on that same day.
3. Forty-nine days after the seventh-day Sabbath following that year's Passover, the Holy Spirit was poured out on the first day of the week, which we know as Shavuot or Pentecost.

Also, there are two instances when the early Messianic church met on the first day of the week:

1. Acts 20:7, the disciples gathered to break bread and to hear Paul teach.
2. First Corinthians 16:2, Paul instructed the collection for the saints in Jerusalem to be gathered on the first day of the week.

We are not explicitly commanded under the New Covenant to attend any church on the first day or any other day, but we are instructed by the apostle Paul not to forsake the gathering of ourselves together (Heb. 10:25). Any day is a good day to gather and seek the Lord, and while the seventh-day Sabbath and the Lord's Day are both scripturally supported, neither should be despised.

Sabbath Considerations

The apostle Paul regularly attended synagogues on the seventh-day Sabbath to proclaim Yeshua Hamashiach as the Messiah to the Jews. Every Sabbath was an appointed time when the nation of Israel would gather and hear the teachers of the Law, and as Paul was tirelessly trying to win over converts to Christ, what better way to witness to Hebrews than on any of the Sabbaths and high holy days. Paul was becoming all things to all men that by any means he might save some.

> And to the Jews I became as a Jew, that I might win Jews; to those who are under the law, as under the law, that I might win those who are under the law; to those who are without law, as without law (not being without law toward God, but under law toward Christ), that I might win those who are without law. (1 Cor. 9:20–21 NKJV)

The Sabbath became a mandatory day of rest by covenant to the Hebrew nation at the giving of the Mosaic Law, a day of cessation from the toils of life with respect to Yehovah's seventh day of rest after His creation. There are instances prior to the giving of the Mosaic Law of certain persons possibly honoring the seventh day, which some believe implies adherence to observing the Sabbath, but none of them mention the seventh day or the Sabbath directly, nor are they referenced as a commandment.

> And Enoch walked with God; and he was not, for God took him. (Gen. 5:24 NKJV)

Some presume this indicates that Enoch kept the seventh day, though there is no other confirming scripture of him observing the seventh day. However, Enoch must have liked spending time with the Father, as he pleased God and did not see death but was taken to heaven (Heb. 11:5). I would expect that the seventh day was just one of many that Enoch spent with the Father. When we delight ourselves in Him, the trappings of this world lose their allure.

In Genesis 6:9, we have another example of an inferred Sabbath observance:

> Noah was a just man, perfect in his generations. (Gen. 6:9 NKJV)

There is no direct reference to the seventh day, only that Noah was just and perfect. It is presumed Noah kept the seventh day based on his character.

And, in speaking with Abraham,

> For I have known him, in order that he may command his children and his household after him, that they keep the way of the Lord, to do righteousness and justice, that the Lord may bring to Abraham what He has spoken to him. (Gen. 18:19 NKJV)

> "Because Abraham obeyed My voice and kept My charge, My commandments, My statutes, and My laws." (Gen. 26:5 NKJV)

Again, the implication that Abraham or any of the forefathers prior to Moses were commanded to keep the seventh day is simply not evidenced in the canonized books of the Holy Bible. These assumptions run counter to the specific references of Nehemiah 9:14 and Deuteronomy 5:2–3, when the Sabbath was made known through Moses and given as a requirement of the covenant.

When considering extrabiblical sources or noncanonized books, such as the book of Jubilees, its instruction to observe the Sabbath is similarly lacking. Let's begin in chapter 1:1 where God called Moses up to the mount, and the glory of the Lord abided on the mount and was clouded over for six days. Then on the seventh day, the glory of the Lord appeared as a flaming fire, and God began to teach Moses for the remaining forty days and nights. During this time, God revealed the Sabbath to Moses, presumably on the seventh day. It does not suggest that the Sabbath was revealed to any of the forefathers at any time prior to Mt. Sinai. Thereafter, in Jubilees 2:18–21,

28, 30, God commanded a Sabbath rest to the seed of Jacob—that is, Israel. Then, in verse 31, it is further clarified that God did not sanctify all peoples and nations to observe the Sabbath but Israel alone. These scriptures indicate that God did not reveal its sanctity to the forefathers, from Adam until the seed of Jacob (Jubilees 2:30), and therefore they may not have kept it. Hence, if a law is not given, then it cannot be applicable to them, even as the apostle Paul writes in Romans 4:15.

> Because the law brings about wrath; for where there is no law there is no transgression. (Rom. 4:15 NKJV)

Moving forward a couple of millennia, the commandment as described in the book of Jubilees, being associated with the Law of Moses, must be considered to have been nailed to the cross (Col. 2:14) along with the rest of the Mosaic Covenant, as the apostle Paul also states that it is a shadow of things to come.

> So let no one judge you in food or in drink, or regarding a festival or a new moon or sabbaths, which are a shadow of things to come, but the substance is of Christ. (Col. 2:16–17 NKJV)

These are all things that were forbidden in the law to eat and drink, or holy days that could not be missed. Again, the substance of every Sabbath and high holy day is Jesus Christ, our Sabbath! Our rest!

In the letter of Luke to Theophilus, in Acts 15:1–2, he relates the actions of the apostles and elders who debated the Gentiles' inclusion into the salvation plan of Yehovah. The Gentile Christians who received the baptism of the Holy Spirit were not commanded to observe the seventh day Sabbath or any high holy day.

> Now therefore, why do you test God by putting a yoke on the neck of the disciples which neither our fathers nor we were able to bear? But we believe that through the grace of the Lord Jesus Christ we shall be saved in the same manner as they. (Acts 15:10–11 NKJV)

The Gentile's salvation was not based on Sabbath keeping or any other tenet of the Law of Moses. In Acts 15:19–21, they were directed to abstain from idols, sexual immorality, things strangled, and blood but nothing regarding the Sabbath. Then again, in verse 24, Paul says that they gave no such commandment to keep the Law. This is clearly not a command to observe the Sabbath's or high holy days.

After the debate, when writing the letter to the church at Antioch, if the apostles had determined that compliance to Sabbath keeping was incumbent on the church, would they have not included it in their charge in Acts 15:28–29?

> For it seemed good to the Holy Spirit, and to us, to lay upon you no greater burden than these necessary things: that you abstain from things offered to idols, from blood, from things strangled, and from sexual immorality. If you keep yourselves from these, you will do well. Farewell. (Acts 15:28–29 NKJV)

Surely, the Sabbath would have been equally as important as these, and if so, why was it not mentioned?

Let's consider for a moment this question. Why would Yehovah impose a commandment on the Gentile believers that neither Adam nor the early patriarchs kept? Adam did not keep the first instruction to not eat of the Tree of Knowledge of Good and Evil. Furthermore, no one kept the Mosaic Commandments perfectly. They all failed except Yeshua Hamashiach.

After Yeshua Hamashiach fulfilled the Old Covenant, He was raised from the dead on the Sabbath! Another good work performed on the Sabbath, as one might surmise that Yeshua's resurrection would have constituted a day of work. Yeshua did many good works on the Sabbath, as He is Lord of the Sabbath, and people needed deliverance from demons, sickness, bondage to sin, and religion. Yeshua performed many miracles on the Sabbath to prove that He had authority over that sanctified day of rest. Only Yehovah could have done that and gotten away with it! So why didn't they believe in Him? Why don't we?

Yehovah has not cast aside the sanctity of the seventh day, as He has never rescinded it. The commandment to observe it according to the

Law of Moses has certainly been set aside. We simply should not observe its adherence as a stricture of the Law of Moses or as a means of our justification. Yehovah made the Sabbath for man, not for Himself. The Sabbath day is a shadow of the eternal rest that Christ has supplied us in Himself. He is Lord of the Sabbath eternally. He is the substance of all the Sabbaths. It is not the Sabbath that makes the Lord holy; it is the Lord Jesus who has become our Sabbath rest and makes us holy. We are not resting in a day; we are resting in the Lord Jesus.

Consider what the apostle Paul is addressing in Galatians 4:10:

> You observe days and months and seasons and years. I am afraid for you, lest I have labored for you in vain. (Gal. 4:10 NKJV)

Paul plainly states that he is afraid for them because they have missed the point. Some state that Paul is referencing the observance of mysticism, pagan calendars, moons, celestial signs, and so on. But look at the preceding verse in Galatians 4:1–4.

> Now I say that the heir, as long as he is a child, does not differ at all from a slave, though he is master of all, but is under guardians and stewards until the time appointed by the father. Even so we, when we were children, were in bondage under the elements of the world. But when the fullness of the time had come, God sent forth His Son, born of a woman, born under the law, to redeem those who were under the law, that we might receive the adoption as sons. (Gal. 4:1–4 NKJV)

Paul is talking about those who were under the Law, those who were slaves to the Law, under bondage, and not about pagan rituals!

Again, in Galatians 4:21, the apostle Paul continues his reference to those who want to be under the Law, those who are of the bondwoman. He clearly is not addressing pagan observance of days, months, seasons, and years. It simply does not fit in the narrative. On the other hand, Paul is not casting off the Sabbath day but rather a system of religious observances as they pertain to justification.

In the first few scriptures of Romans, chapter 14, Paul is once again addressing our liberty—liberty to eat all things or not, or to observe one day as greater than another. Paul is speaking of items in the Mosaic Law, as he has no regard for pagan rituals.

> One person esteems one day above another; another esteems every day alike. Let each be fully convinced in his own mind. He who observes the day, observes it to the Lord; and he who does not observe the day, to the Lord he does not observe it. (Rom. 14:5–6 NKJV)

Here is another good opportunity for the apostle Paul to bind the observance of the Sabbath on the Christian. What other day of observance could he possibly be referring to? But he did not, nor is it found in any other book of the New Covenant. If a fellow Christian desires to sanctify the Sabbath or the Lord's Day, no one is to refrain them from serving the Lord Yeshua. They are observing them as unto the Lord. On the other hand, the apostle Paul also stated that if one does not esteem or observe one day above the other, that is fine too. One might consider not to quarrel over such opinions (Rom. 14:1).

When the new heaven and the new earth are created, night will no longer exist (Rev. 22:5). Yehovah will give us clear direction on what to do at that time. For a certainty, this present heaven and earth will one day pass away (Matt. 24:35), and our substance, our dwelling place, will remain Christ Jesus. We are to be at peace beloved. The curse of the Law has been lifted, as the Law of Moses, its ordinances and commandments, that enmity that resulted in our cursing, have been abolished for our benefit (Heb. 10:9, Eph. 2:14–16).

Lord of the Sabbath

There is another declaration we must consider. Yeshua Hamashiach declared that He is the Lord of the Sabbath. When we rest in Him, we are resting in His eternal Sabbath (rest).

"Yet I say to you that in this place there is One greater than the temple. But if you had known what this means, I desire mercy and not sacrifice,' you would not have condemned the guiltless. For the Son of Man is Lord even of the Sabbath." (Matt. 12:6–8 NKJV)

Yeshua Hamashiach is greater than the giving of the Law of Moses on Mt. Sinai (Heb. 3:3), He is greater than the temple, greater than the heavens and the earth that He created, and He is greater than the seventh day! When we abide in Him, we are abiding in His rest (Col. 1:17).

Jesus is saying several different things here:

1. Yeshua references himself as a priest, likened to the priest who served the earthly temple in Matthew 12:6. He proclaims that He is one greater than not only the priests but also of the physical temple of Jerusalem.

2. While the disciples were plucking (harvesting) heads of grain on the Sabbath, Jesus replied to the Pharisees that He desired mercy to be shown (Matt. 12:1–2). Similarly, in John 9:16, Yeshua is condemned by the Pharisees for not keeping the seventh-day Sabbath because He healed a blind man. In John 5, Jesus healed the lame man at the pool of Bethesda on the Sabbath, and the Jews sought to kill him. But more astonishing than this, Yeshua says, "My Father has been working until now, and I have been working" (John 5:17 NKJV). There are many scriptures where Jesus is working and doing good on the seventh day (Mark 3:4, Luke 6:6–11, John 5:10).

3. When the priests served in the temple on the Sabbath, they were working but were not held guilty (Matt. 12:5). Yeshua created the fields and grew the grain, and as Lord of the Sabbath, He would soon purchase the redemption of His disciples, making us part of His body (Col. 1:18). Indeed, the priests were guiltless as per God's command, just as we are guiltless by like faith in Him. Just as Abraham believed God and just as David was guiltless for taking the showbread because he looked forward to the promised Messiah who would redeem Israel. Yeshua created and met the requirements

for righteousness and obedience to the Law, qualifying Himself in righteousness as our Sabbath.

> We have an altar from which those who serve the tabernacle have no right to eat. (Heb. 13:8 NKJV)

Yeshua Hamashiach is the fulfillment of the Law, and He is the High Priest of the New Covenant.

4. The Son of Man is Lord even of the Sabbath. Jesus is preeminent to the Sabbath commandments given in Exodus 20:8–11 and 31:14. He is preeminent to the Mosaic Covenant even as He is preeminent to the New Covenant and to all eternity. He, being the Word of Yehovah manifest in the flesh, created the seventh day and established it within Himself.

    > And He is the head of the body, the church, who is the beginning, the firstborn from the dead, that in all things He may have the preeminence. (Col. 1:18 NKJV)

    When He says, "Come to Me, all you who labor and are heavy laden, and I will give you rest" (Matt. 11:28 NKJV), naturally He is speaking of abiding within Yeshua Hamashiach. And what burden were they carrying that they should be delivered from? It was the Law of Sin and Death, the Law of Moses, and their inability to keep it. He is speaking of eternal rest from sin, trouble, failure, and the Law by abiding in Him.

5. The New Covenant is a better covenant that requires a better sacrifice than bulls and goats; we must accept its authority! Yeshua Hamashiach established it for us! In Israel today, there is a renewed commitment to build a third temple. Many Christians are in support of its institution and are enamored with the ark of the covenant and the copies of those holy implements in heaven. There is great danger in the idolatrous observance of icons, rites,

and rituals in our attempts to justify ourselves before Yehovah. He destroyed the physical temple for our instruction! Yeshua is the priest of a better covenant that is in heaven, not Jerusalem.

> For Christ has not entered the holy places made with hands, which are copies of the true, but into heaven itself, now to appear in the presence of God for us. (Heb. 9:23–24 NKJV)

I like to work and be productive, and other days I like a day of rest, but eventually we all get weary of working and striving for our existence, and we seek rest. Is that not what we are looking for—a continual place of peace and rest? Though the Sabbath requirement was never imposed on the forefathers by covenant with life-and-death conditions (Adam, Enoch, Noah, or Abraham), we can reasonably assume they knew of the seventh day, its sanctity, and its lack of additional stipulations, as none are recorded or can be found. On the other hand, in Deuteronomy 5, only the children at Mt. Horeb are so commanded:

> The Lord our God made a covenant with us in Horeb. The Lord did not make this covenant with our fathers, but with us, those who are here today, all of us who are alive. (Deut. 5:2–3 NKJV)

This proof confirms that the forefathers were not under the Mosaic Covenant. That's a big difference, my friends (Neh. 9:14).

Let's consider more:

1. The Father's creation of the seventh day of rest in Genesis 2:2–3, wherein He rested and blessed the seventh day, is significant because Father foreknew the design, purpose, and glory of the seventh day. Just as all the celestial bodies have meaning and a set course, the Sabbath, too, was determined with purpose and not just an extra day. Yehovah had predetermined a more particular event for it. The question is what was His intended plan? God did not need to rest. He created the seventh-day Sabbath for man (Mark

2:27). God created the seventh day to mark as a future Sabbath for the children of Israel, the conclusion of six days of labor. A foreshadowing of a rest in Messiah and of a future consumption of this earth with fire, bringing it to its end, that He may create a new heaven and a new earth (Rev. 21:1), having no curse or night (Rev. 22:3, 5), one eternal day.

2. When considering Yehovah's charge to Adam in the garden, we go back to a time before sin corrupted the Father's creation. Adam and Eve walked in the garden, tending and keeping it (Gen. 2:15), exercising dominion and authority over all the earth (Gen. 1:26). There is no mention of them observing the seventh day, presumably because they did not need a day of rest, as they walked with God each day. They were, however, commanded not to eat of the Tree of Knowledge of Good and Evil lest they die (Gen. 2:17). We must acknowledge that they were not instructed to keep the seventh day lest they should die. It's a conundrum for the Sabbatarian to explain why those who have been redeemed by the New Covenant should be so constrained by Mosaic Law when Yeshua has become our eternal rest. We can continue to honor the seventh day as Adam, Enoch, Noah, and Abram may have done. Again, however, they were never instructed to keep it per commandment, thus avoiding the predication of judgment for its noncompliance. We may continue observing the seventh day of rest as it continues to speak of Christ Jesus as our eternal rest, just as all the high holy day Sabbaths speak of Yeshua. We need only avoid the pretext of its use as a justification by works per the Mosaic Law since Yeshua Hamashiach has become our righteousness (2 Cor. 5:17, 21).

3. The Sabbath observance is incorporated into the Mosaic Covenant's Decalogue as the Fourth Commandment to remember it and keep holy (Exod. 20:8 and Deut. 5:12). These are addressed specifically to the children of Israel at Mt. Horeb. This covenant, however, was not applicable to the pagan or Gentile nations but only for the children of Jacob. However, does it still exist as a standing commandment to those who choose to live under the Law of Moses? The book of Romans tells us that some will be judged according to the Law, and others will be judged who lived without

the Law (Rom. 2:12). Considering that this instruction was given after the New Covenant had been instituted, the Mosaic Law can still be adhered to if one so agrees, much as those who were under the Law since Mt. Horeb. Those who choose not to believe in the Messiah will be judged according to their legal standing in relation to the Mosaic Law. Similarly, the Gentile unbeliever will be judged according to their conscience, yet outside the covenant redemption and protection of Christ Jesus (Rom. 2:14–16). And as for the professing Christian who insists on keeping any aspect of the Law of Moses as justification, Galatians 5:2 will apply; Christ will profit you nothing!

> Stand fast therefore in the liberty by which Christ has made us free, and do not be entangled again with a yoke of bondage. Indeed I, Paul, say to you that if you become circumcised, Christ will profit you nothing. And I testify again to every man who becomes circumcised that he is a debtor to keep the whole law. You have become estranged from Christ, you who attempt to be justified by law; you have fallen from grace. (Gal. 5:1–4 NKJV)

This is the Gospel, the Good News, the liberating news that Paul and all the apostles preached and for which they were put to death. Some people prefer bondage, laws, and religious self-justification and will go to great lengths to make misery of their own lives and to condemn those who choose liberty in Yeshua Hamashiach.

4. There is a Sabbath rest as a shadow of things to come in Colossians 2:17 that envelops all seventh-day Sabbaths, high holy day Sabbaths, and the Lord's Day.

> So let no one judge you in food or in drink, or regarding a festival or a new moon or sabbaths, which are a shadow of things to come, but the substance is of Christ. (Col. 2:16–17 NKJV)

Paul is referring to the completed view of the redemptive state for those who have accepted Messiah. Consider the importance of a Sabbath once this heaven and earth are consumed by fire and Father creates a new heaven and a new earth. Would we still observe Sabbaths of an old earth that no longer exists? Would He not restore our fellowship with Him back to what existed prior to the Fall of Adam and Eve? For a certainty, He would do no less! Neither will foods or drink be regarded as clean or unclean in the new heaven and earth. God is moving our mindset from the temporal tabernacle at Jerusalem to the eternal. Though the life of the flesh is in the blood (Lev. 17:11) and countless millions of bulls and goats were sacrificed for an inadequate temporary sanctification (Heb. 10:4, 11), and though some may offer blood sacrifices in ignorance or in memorial, once our Messiah was sacrificed, He alone became our eternal sanctification. Henceforth, all animal blood atonement sacrifices were rendered ineffective, even offensive to His abundant mercy.

> For by one offering He has perfected forever those who are being sanctified. (Heb. 10:14 NKJV)

> Having wiped out the handwriting of requirements that was against us, which was contrary to us. And He has taken it out of the way, having nailed it to the cross. (Col. 2:14 NKJV)

Yeshua Hamashiach supposedly broke the Sabbath in Matthew 12:4. However, when one considers that He deliberately performed works on the Sabbath, it was done to proclaim His authority, that He alone is Lord of the Sabbath Day (Matt. 12:8). He is the Lord and Creator of the Sabbath. His actions on any Sabbath are contained within His own authority, and none can question it. Those who promote the Sabbath are extolling its supremacy over the one who made it! They extol it over the promise that Yehovah made to Abram, a promise given prior to the Law, prior to the observance of the seven different Sabbath's given in Lev. 23.

Abram simply believed and trusted God's promise. We also find that doing good on the Sabbath is the very essence of observing the Sabbath, whether under the Law or not, in that resting, healing, bringing deliverance to another, taking the showbread as David did, or plucking heads of grain on the Sabbath glorifies Yehovah and is not a violation, when one believes they are accepted in Yeshua Hamashiach.

> Knowing that a man is not justified by the works of the law but by faith in Jesus Christ, even we have believed in Christ Jesus, that we might be justified by faith in Christ and not by the works of the law; for by the works of the law no flesh shall be justified. (Gal. 2:16 NKJV)

> "But that no one is justified by the law in the sight of God is evident, for "the just shall live by faith." Yet the law is not of faith, but "the man who does them shall live by them." Christ has redeemed us from the curse of the law, having become a curse for us (for it is written, "Cursed is everyone who hangs on a tree"), that the blessing of Abraham might come upon the Gentiles in Christ Jesus, that we might receive the promise of the Spirit through faith. (Gal. 3:11–14 NKJV)

Dire Consequences of Unbelief

In Hebrews 3:16–19, we see that the children of Israel rebelled against the commandment of Yehovah to enter the promised land. They could not enter in because of unbelief! Paul then ties this epic event of unbelief to those of his ministry who heard the Gospel but received no profit from it because they did not mix it with faith (Heb. 4:1–2)! Fortunately, there is a promise to those who do believe in the Messiah, "for we who have believed do enter that rest" (Heb. 4:3 NKJV).

Some theorize that that entering in is some time in the future; however, the past tense of "have believed" signifies a preceding act of faith that qualifies the present action "do enter." Entering His rest today is further supported by Christ's promise of Matthew 11:28 and John 14:27. "Peace I leave with you, my peace I give to you" (John 14:27 NKJV). Well, did He leave it with us, or did He lie about it? It is on us to accept the peace that He gives and to enter His rest.

You may ask, "How can we be assured of His peace in us?" We back up a few verses to John 14:21–23 for another simple Christ truth:

> "He who has My commandments and keeps them, it is he who loves Me. And he who loves Me will be loved by My Father, and I will love him and manifest Myself to him." Judas (not Iscariot) said to Him, "Lord, how is it that You will manifest Yourself to us, and not to the world?" Jesus answered and said to him, "If anyone loves Me, he will keep My word; and My Father will love him, and We will come to him and make Our home with him." (John 14:21–23 NKJV)

This, my friends, is true rest, to have your home with Him today! We need not look any further for strictures or commands to enter His rest.

What is God's commandment to us today? Paul, in writing to Timothy, gives a commandment:

> That you may charge some that they teach no other doctrine, nor give heed to fables and endless genealogies, which cause disputes rather than godly edification which is in faith. (1 Tim. 1:3–4 NKJV)

He is speaking of faith in Messiah's work on the cross, the confirmation and consummation of the New Covenant, our present-day eternal rest. Then:

> Now the purpose of the commandment is love from a pure heart, from a good conscience, and from sincere faith. (1 Tim. 1:5 NKJV)

And, of course, the Lord's preeminent commandment in Matthew 22:37–40.

When we enter in and accept Yeshua Hamashiach, we also cease from a works justification. Let's back up a bit to Hebrews 4:8–10 in reference to Joshua, who took over leading the children of Israel after Moses died. He also did not give them rest.

> For if Joshua had given them rest, then He would not afterward have spoken of another day. There remains therefore a rest for the people of God. For he who has entered His rest has himself also ceased from his works as God did from His. (Heb. 4:8–10 NKJV)

Have you entered His rest yet, or are you still trying to work yourself into it?

God was not weary after His creation. He chose to rest for our benefit, to appoint a time foreshadowing Moses's commandment and the rest we receive through Christ's redemptive work. Yehovah ceased from His works, even as we also cease from the works of the law and rest in Messiah.

> For we who have believed do enter that rest. (Heb. 4:3 NKJV)

Christ Jesus has become both our Sabbath rest and our eternal rest. So when and how do we enter this rest? Hebrews 4:7 states clearly when and how:

> "Today, if you will hear His voice, do not harden your hearts." (Heb. 4:7 NKJV)

That is, do not harden your heart with unbelief.

> Let us therefore be diligent to enter that rest, lest anyone fall according to the same example of disobedience. (Heb. 4:11 NKJV)

We too, must continue to exercise our faith in His promise, to exercise diligence lest we fall "according to the same example of disobedience."

That disobedience is unbelief (Hebrews 3:18–19)! There is no diligence demonstrated here to keep the Law or serve the temple. Those things had been set aside, even rendered physically useless by Yehovah Himself. We must enter His rest by faith in the work of Christ Jesus.

> Jesus said to her, "Woman, believe Me, the hour is coming when you will neither on this mountain, nor in Jerusalem, worship the Father. You worship what you do not know; we know what we worship, for salvation is of the Jews. But the hour is coming, and now is, when the true worshipers will worship the Father in spirit and truth; for the Father is seeking such to worship Him. God is Spirit, and those who worship Him must worship in spirit and truth." (John 4:21–24 NKJV)

This scripture beloved is the Father's encouragement to move our mindset from the old religious ideals to worshipping the Father in the Holy Spirt and truth. Whether it be the seventh day, the first day, or any other, our Father is to be honored always.

We have come full circle from being created in the image of Yehovah, to falling in Adam, then through the Law as being incapable, and now back again in Christ Jesus to become worshippers of Him in spirit and truth. He does not seek us to meet Him in any other temple than the one He creates within us. Our worship is not relegated to a physical location or any specific day. It is only done in the spirit and in truth.

Today, there is a resurgence by legalists to press for observance of some aspects of the Torah, in so much that they try to keep the Sabbath's by observances and abstaining from any work. The Sabbath's have once again become a law to some professing Christians, laws that neither Adam, Abram nor Gentiles, were ever under in the first place. Then, on the opposite end of the spectrum, there is the required church attendance on the Lord's Day, as though it, too, were now a New Covenant commandment law, every bit as imposing and compulsory as the Mosaic Sabbath, and/or that the Lord's Day has now replaced the Sabbath. There are implications being taught in churches today that select portions of the Law of Moses and the book of the Law (Genesis through Deuteronomy) must still be observed, engendering a sense of doom if those portions of the Torah are not obeyed. Some even levy a curse against others for noncompliance. Oddly, they neglect to identify precisely which OT commands remain applicable and which are no longer in force; just the mere suggestion of its applicability is generally enough to quell any dissent. Circumcision and blood sacrifices are routinely exempted from observances, but Sabbath days, the Lord's Day, and the tithe appear to remain sacrosanct. A lack of New Covenant understanding is clear.

Modern-day Pharisees have instituted legalism, liturgies, religious systems, and bylaws that are to be followed lest scorn be dispensed. Sadly, some legalists consider attendance at the religious edifice as the true definition of keeping the Lord's Day or Sabbath. We have replaced worshipping in spirit and truth with the axiom of religious duty. Paul addressed this to Timothy and gave this instruction:

> Now the purpose of the commandment is love from a pure
> heart, from a good conscience, and from sincere faith, from
> which some, having strayed, have turned aside to idle talk,
> desiring to be teachers of the law, understanding neither
> what they say nor the things which they affirm. (1 Tim.
> 1:5–7 NKJV)

By not accepting Christ Jesus's full atonement and justification for their souls, these hapless teachers of the law condemn themselves.

Mandated weekly church building attendance was not an aspect of Yehovah's divine appointment in the Garden of Eden, nor by the forefathers up until Moses, nor by the first-century Christians, nor by New Testament commandment. The Mosaic Law required observance of the Sabbath (seventh day), but it is quite the opposite of today's Sunday services. Even the title, Sunday, is an affront to righteousness, as it is named in honor of Babylonian, Greek, and Roman sun gods that have been worshipped for millennia. Suffice it to say that we probably won't be referring to it as the first day of the week anytime soon, though we should. Notwithstanding, if the Sabbath Day, as exercised on the seventh day, were still in force, then Christians have been missing it for nearly two thousand years.

On the Sabbath, the children of Israel would stay at home to rest, pray, and meditate or stroll over to the local synagogue if it were not too far. Violating the prohibitions of the Sabbath could hold a death sentence if violated by working on it or by not honoring it. By contrast, today, if you attempt to rest at home on the Lord's Day, read, pray, and do no labor, you may arise suspicions of being a rebel, a potential backslider with questionable commitment.

When growing up, our efforts to attend services on the Lord's Day were a hurried attempt to corral seven kids into clothes, food, and car, which in no way resembled anything like rest. Upon arriving early for Sunday school, the stresses of duty, protocols, attendance, and doctrinal compliance were a high priority. After church, my mother would finish cooking lunch, which she had started earlier, before breakfast. Then cleaning the mess hall was another hour. Hopefully, after the mayhem, we had time for a nap before getting prepared to go back to the evening services for more denominational courtesies. Who had time to relax, pray, study the scriptures, and truly seek the Lord? Yeshua's work to set mankind at liberty and rest and to worship Him in spirit and truth was once again supplanted by religious systems and doctrines of men. We had little clue what the Sabbath Day had been intended to provide; mostly, as we understood it, it had now moved to Sunday. We had unwittingly shown disrespect to the Father's New Covenant by not resting in Christ's finished work, our justification by His grace. We have insulted the Spirit of Grace through our busyness, our religious works of self-justification, ignorance, and unbelief. It was for freedom that Christ set us free, to be freed from the Law, from its ordinances that we could not keep, and from the power of sin, which received its authority from that Law. Through our vain attempt, we did not recognize our liberty to enter Christ's perpetual and eternal rest.

"Come to Me, all you who labor and are heavy laden, and
I will give you rest." (Matt. 11:28 NKJV)

Over the decades, I discovered that all the other denominations out there were just as misguided as our own, some even worse. Church families were a whole lot like our own imperfect brood of nine. Of course, we didn't think ourselves as imperfect—well, at least not by much. Our devotion, despite our familial imperfection and our adherence to religious duties, blinded us, robbing us of the Gospel and the liberty Yeshua Hamashiach gave us. Thankfully, through it all, Christ Jesus was preached, and somehow, quite literally by the grace of Yehovah and the persistence of the Holy Spirit, His grace broke through!

> Stand fast therefore in the liberty by which Christ has made us free, and do not be entangled again with a yoke of bondage. Indeed I, Paul, say to you that if you become circumcised, Christ will profit you nothing. (Gal. 5:1–2 NKJV)

Circumcision was a sign of the covenant that Yehovah made with Abraham and his descendants. It was symbolic of cutting away the carnal nature of man, man's desire for effecting life by his own work and strength. The children of Israel have long held onto the law of circumcision as their sign of being Yehovah's chosen people and of His promise; it remains the central tenet of their faith. When the apostle Paul began to preach Christ as their Messiah and of our liberty in Christ apart from the works of the Law, of which circumcision is primary, they became enraged and persecuted Christian believers. The Law of Moses proved to us that our works are insufficient to meet Yehovah's demand for perfection, and therefore, Christ was determined to become our righteousness (2 Cor. 5:21).

> Not forsaking the assembling of ourselves together, as is the manner of some. (Heb. 10:25 NKJV)

This is the mantra of many Christian organizations, I suppose to keep us well taught, groomed, and regularly attending. Mostly, however, it became a criterion for the faithful; miss a Sunday or Wednesday-night service, and your Christianity was suspect but tolerable. Miss a Sunday without a substantial excuse, and you were on the fringe of apostasy. We Gentile Christians probably need instruction more than our Hebrew counterparts, simply because we start off on the wrong foot and are forever trying to catch up with the Hebrew culture. Fellowship with other Christians is essential to the Christian life. We need one another. The gifts and ministries that Yehovah has placed in the body of Christ are given for our edification, comfort, and growth. Let's engage them frequently.

> Do you not know that you are the temple of God and that the Spirit of God dwells in you? If anyone defiles the temple of God, God will destroy him. For the temple of God is holy, which temple you are. (1 Cor. 3:16–17 NKJV)

We do not serve the temple at Jerusalem, nor do we serve the church building on the corner; we serve the abiding presence of Christ Jesus in our hearts. Yehovah is not concerned with physical temples but with His righteousness in us, His ever-present Holy Spirit in the hearts of mankind. As we live and breathe, we as temples of Yehovah, carrying about within us the Spirit of God, being one in the body of Christ Jesus, do we still need to observe a Sabbath Day on the seventh day, or are we to be continually dwelling in His rest?

We can still fulfill the requirements of what the Law was teaching but by a better covenant.

> Owe no one anything except to love one another, for he who loves another has fulfilled the law. For the commandments, "You shall not commit adultery," "You shall not murder," "You shall not steal," "You shall not bear false witness," "You shall not covet," and if there is any other commandment, are all summed up in this saying, namely, "You shall love your neighbor as yourself." Love does no harm to a neighbor; therefore, love is the fulfillment of the law. (Rom. 13:8–10 NKJV)

So did any of these commandments pass away? Clearly, no. But are they levied once again in the New Covenant with an adjoining blessing and curse as according to a law unto justification? They cannot justify us before Yehovah. Only Yeshua's atonement qualifies us as righteous. However, they are incorporated in the law of love and cannot be denied. Can we say today that the Sabbath has been set aside? The summation of this discussion is that you cannot set aside that in which you are eternally dwelling; that is, when you are dwelling in Christ Jesus, you are dwelling within Sabbath rest.

And if there are any other commandments remaining that may need to be considered, they, too, are fulfilled according to the law of love (Mat. 22:37) and the Law of the Spirit of Life (Rom. 8:2), that we may accept the legal requirements of the Mosaic Law as being fulfilled by Christ and that the sanctity of the seventh day abides wholly in Yeshua Hamashiach, our Messiah, our eternal rest.

CHAPTER 14

BE LED BY THE HOLY SPIRIT

The Holy Spirit will reveal the word of truth to those who seek truth. An abiding presence of peace and confidence will accompany His direction to your soul. On occasion, He will direct us in a way that appears difficult, one that may go against our limited knowledge or preference, but His peace will remain with us, never forsaking us. Without exception, the Word of Yehovah never contradicts itself but always provides recurring themes regarding His will. If your view of being led by the Spirit of Yehovah needs clarification, you will find it in the Word of Yehovah. There are many false prophets today, and one must measure their utterances by the authority of the Word; anything outside of the written Word should be rejected. You are going to lose friends and incur enemies over scriptural authority. The sincere Christian must prepare themselves with a solid study in the Word of God (2 Tim. 2:15).

> "However, when He, the Spirit of truth, has come, He will guide you into all truth; for He will not speak on His own authority, but whatever He hears He will speak; and He will tell you things to come. He will glorify Me, for He will take of what is Mine and declare it to you." (John 16:13–14 NKJV)

> "You search the Scriptures, for in them you think you have eternal life; and these are they which testify of Me. But you

are not willing to come to Me that you may have life." (John 5:39–40 NKJV)

The scriptures testify that Yeshua Hamashiach is our Sabbath rest, our liberator from the Law, our righteousness. If we search scripture to prove our doctrinal bias, it will only lead to blindness. We must commune with the Father to hear His voice and allow the Holy Spirit to bring us revelation. His instruction will never counter the written Word of Yehovah. His word will reveal wisdom to us and weave a pattern of understanding as we search the scriptures. If any doctrine is incongruent with the redemptive plan of Yehovah's grace and mercy, it is to be rejected.

> For as many as are led by the Spirit of God, these are sons of God. For you did not receive the spirit of bondage again to fear, but you received the Spirit of adoption by whom we cry out, "Abba, Father." (Rom. 8:14–15 NKJV)

The premise of this scripture lies in the statement, "you did not receive the spirit of bondage again to fear." Beloved, if what you are hearing in your spirit is leading you back to legalism, fear, condemnation, or despair, you can reject it outright! The Holy Spirit will always bring you into the truth of the word and will of Yehovah. Guaranteed! So, remain at peace and ask Him for understanding.

> But the wisdom that is from above is first pure, then peaceable, gentle, willing to yield, full of mercy and good fruits, without partiality and without hypocrisy. (James 3:17 NKJV)

Jesus proclaimed that the scriptures testified of Himself as the Creator and God of our salvation and as the physical manifestation of Yehovah's Word (John 1:1–3). We are not to worship scripture, edifices, or theological dissertation but Him who creates all things and gives life freely. Every thought we once considered as our own cognition and theory were known by Him before we existed in human form, as there is nothing new under the sun to Yehovah. Our freedom to choose remains our own. We either believe in His absolute sovereignty or we vainly deceive ourselves. We can only agree with His dominion or rebel against it, or will the thing formed say to its Creator, "You have no hands?" (Rom. 9:21 NKJV).

We can choose to be filled with works of death or filled with the Word of Yehovah, which is Yeshua. The Father's desire is to manifest His nature, Spirit, and presence through us. All that He creates is done in purity and perfection. We are an extension of His being and glory. There is no other perfect, holy, and righteous entity that can manifest through us. Yehovah alone exists as the great I Am. All things are created by and for His divine will (John 1:3).

We must remember that our dwelling place is not of this earth, not in a building or assembly but in the person of Yeshua Hamashiach, and that our righteousness comes not through obedience to the Mosaic Law but from His grace alone.

> For I through the law died to the law that I might live to God. I have been crucified with Christ; it is no longer I who live, but Christ lives in me; and the life which I now live in the flesh I live by faith in the Son of God, who loved me and gave Himself for me. I do not set aside the grace of God; for if righteousness comes through the law, then Christ died in vain. (Gal. 2:19–21 NKJV)

This is the Good News of Jesus Christ!

> Now when He was asked by the Pharisees when the kingdom of God would come, He answered them and said, "The kingdom of God does not come with observation; nor will they say, 'See here!' or 'See there!' For indeed, the kingdom of God is within you." (Luke 17:20–21 NKJV)

If indeed we are being led by the Holy Spirit, how then are we to observe His coming? We do not seek an earthly kingdom but an eternal presence with the Spirit of Yehovah in our hearts. Our faith confirms His power in us.

> Whom having not seen you love. Though now you do not
> see Him, yet believing, you rejoice with joy inexpressible
> and full of glory, receiving the end of your faith—the
> salvation of your souls. (1 Pet. 1:8–9 NKJV)

Heretical teaching will deprive the sincere Christian of Christ's life-giving Spirit to live through them. Jesus came to set the captives free—free from the sin that had its power in the Law; free from the confines of the Mosaic Law, which even the apostles and the Hebrew forefathers were unable to keep; and hence, freedom from the sting of death (Rom. 7:8). Yehovah intentionally made the Mosaic Law and all the prophecies regarding Messiah so complicated and impossible to keep that there could be no misunderstanding that only Yehovah Himself could fulfill them. And fulfill them He did.

> And release those who through fear of death were all their
> lifetime subject to bondage. (Heb. 2:15 NKJV)

We are free to live life without the fear of offending or displeasing the Father. His Holy Spirit leads us into all truth and teaches us, guiding our steps toward holiness. Condemnation is none of the devil's business any longer (Rom. 8:1).

Because of Christ Jesus's sacrifice, we are free to love Yehovah like the woman whose sins were many and who washed His feet with her tears and wiped them with the hair of her head and who did not cease to kiss His feet (Luke 7:44–51). Her heart was enthralled by His presence and perpetual love as she received without effort or cost His absolute forgiveness and acceptance. She knew the merciful heart of Yehovah through Messiah! She had been set free to worship and to rejoice in Him for who He is. She trusted, like Abram, in the one who spoke to her some of the most beautiful words given:

> "Your sins are forgiven." (Luke 7:48 NKJV)

This compelling story displays for us how to love according to Matthew 22:37–40, that when we believe in the efficacy of Christ's atonement and forgiveness of all we have done and accept His eternal love, we, too, will love Him with abandon and serve Him joyously.

> "'You shall love the Lord your God with all your heart, with all your soul, and with all your mind.' This is the first and great commandment. And the second is like it: You shall love your neighbor as yourself.' On these two commandments hang all the Law and the Prophets." (Matt. 22:37–40 NKJV)

This command preceded all other covenants and commandments. It is preeminent among all commands. It is the very power, glory, and substance of Yehovah borne about all His creation. It was the rebellion in the garden, wickedness in the days of Noah, the abominations extant in the Hebrews in bondage and the fallen world combined that compelled the Father through love for His creation to move and save His creation by the holiest of all sacrifices, His only begotten Son.

> What man is he that feareth the Lord? him shall he teach in the way that he shall choose. His soul shall dwell at ease; and his seed shall inherit the earth. The secret of the Lord is with them that fear him; *and he will shew them his covenant.* (Ps. 25:12–14 NKJV; italics by author)

I trust and pray that that is you! To trust in Yehovah's covenant, to know and understand that He is setting His children free, to rejoice in Him, to comfort and keep you for His own delight and kingdom purpose!

> If anyone thinks himself to be a prophet or spiritual, let him acknowledge that the things which I write to you are the commandments of the Lord. But if anyone is ignorant, let him be ignorant. (1 Cor. 14:37–38 NKJV)

As the apostle Paul penned these words, we must remember that his instructions were not based on personal or denominational bias but on the leading of the Holy Spirit. Though some of these verses may disturb our theological bent, they define the promises and covenants as they transitioned from one to another, supplied to us through Yehovah's mercy and grace, that we may grow in the liberty of Christ Jesus to love and honor our Father in spirit and truth. Yehovah's plan, purchase, and purpose was a reformation of covenants, that we might become one.

O' what a beautiful Savior!

May Father's grace and peace be with your spirit.

Yours in Christ,
Brother Ken

Printed in the United States
by Baker & Taylor Publisher Services